HYSTERIA TODAY

THE CENTRE FOR FREUDIAN ANALYSIS AND RESEARCH LIBRARY

Series Editors:
Anouchka Grose, Darian Leader, Alan Rowan

CFAR was founded in 1985 with the aim of developing Freudian and Lacanian psychoanalysis in the UK. Lacan's rereading and rethinking of Freud had been neglected in the Anglophone world, despite its important implications for the theory and practice of psychoanalysis. Today, this situation is changing, with a lively culture of training groups, seminars, conferences, and publications.

CFAR offers both introductory and advanced courses in psychoanalysis, as well as a clinical training programme in Lacanian psychoanalysis. It can provide access to Lacanian psychoanalysts working in the UK, and has links with Lacanian groups across the world. The CFAR Library aims to make classic Lacanian texts available in English for the first time, as well as publishing original research in the Lacanian field.

OTHER TITLES IN THE SERIES

- *Lacan and Lévi-Strauss or The Return to Freud (1951–1957)*
  by Markos Zafiropoulos
- *The Trainings of the Psychoanalyst*
  by Annie Tardits
- *Sexual Ambiguities*
  by Geneviève Morel
- *Freud and the Desire of the Psychoanalyst*
  by Serge Cottet
- *Lacan: The Unconscious Reinvented*
  by Colette Soler
- *Introductory Lectures on Lacan*
  edited by Astrid Gessert
- *Premature Birth: The Baby, the Doctor, and the Psychoanalyst*
  by Colette Soler

www.cfar.org.uk

HYSTERIA TODAY

Edited by
Anouchka Grose

LONDON AND NEW YORK

First published 2016 by Karnac Books Ltd.

Published 2018 by Routledge
2 Park Square, Milton Park, Abingdon, Oxon OX14 4RN
711 Third Avenue, New York, NY 10017, USA

Routledge is an imprint of the Taylor & Francis Group, an informa business

Copyright © 2016 to Anouchka Grose for the edited collection, and to the individual authors for their contributions.

The rights of the contributors to be identified as the authors of this work have been asserted in accordance with §§ 77 and 78 of the Copyright Design and Patents Act 1988.

All rights reserved. No part of this book may be reprinted or reproduced or utilised in any form or by any electronic, mechanical, or other means, now known or hereafter invented, including photocopying and recording, or in any information storage or retrieval system, without permission in writing from the publishers.

Notice:
Product or corporate names may be trademarks or registered trademarks, and are used only for identification and explanation without intent to infringe.

British Library Cataloguing in Publication Data

A C.I.P. for this book is available from the British Library

ISBN-13: 9781782201045 (pbk)

Typeset by V Publishing Solutions Pvt Ltd., Chennai, India

For Dot

CONTENTS

ACKNOWLEDGEMENTS ix

ABOUT THE CONTRIBUTORS xi

INTRODUCTION
Reclaiming hysteria xv
Anouchka Grose

CHAPTER ONE
Hysterics today 1
Leonardo S. Rodríguez

CHAPTER TWO
Hysteria today 27
Darian Leader

CHAPTER THREE
Beyond queer? 35
Anne Worthington

CHAPTER FOUR
Necessity and seduction: a section of hysteria 53
Vincent Dachy

CHAPTER FIVE
Fifty shades of literary success: the vampire's appeal 63
Geneviève Morel

CHAPTER SIX
Hysteria, a hystory 85
Colette Soler

CHAPTER SEVEN
… As if I did not know … (Allurement) 99
Vincent Dachy

INDEX 103

ACKNOWLEDGEMENTS

Enormous thanks to all the contributors for their hard work. Also to Kristina Valendinova for her skill and generosity, and to Lewis Kerfane for last-minute editing help. Thanks to Darian Leader for suggesting the idea in the first place, and to Oliver Rathbone for saying "yes" to it. Also, to Rod Tweedy and Constance Govindin for their patience. To my parents, of course, and especially to Martin Creed and Dot Grose Forrester.

ABOUT THE CONTRIBUTORS

Vincent Dachy practices and teaches Lacanian psychoanalysis in London. He is a member of the Centre for Freudian Analysis and Research (CFAR) and of the New Lacanian School. Aside from psychoanalysis he writes texts in association with photographs, and reciprocally between prose and poetry. His publications include: *Tribulations of a Westerner in the Western World* (2007) and *Scraps from the Bottom of My Pocket: Bywords in Flexions* (Artwords Press, 2013).

Anouchka Grose is a psychoanalyst and writer practicing in London. She is a member of CFAR and The College of Psychoanalysts UK. She has written non-fiction: *No More Silly Love Songs: A Realist's Guide to Romance* (Portobello, 2010) and *Are You Considering Therapy?* (Karnac, 2011), as well as fiction: *Ringing for You* (Harper Collins, 1999) and *Darling Daisy* (Harper Collins, 2000). She also writes for *The Guardian* and teaches at Camberwell School of Art.

Darian Leader is a psychoanalyst working in London and a founder member of CFAR. He is visiting professor at the School of Human and Life Sciences, Roehampton University. He is the author of several books including: *Introducing Lacan; Why Do Women Writer More Letters Than They Post?; Freud's Footnotes; Stealing the Mona Lisa: What Art Stops Us From Seeing; Why Do People Get Ill* (with David Corfield); *The New Black: Mourning, Melancholia and Depression; What is Madness?;* and *Strictly Bipolar.*

Geneviève Morel is a psychoanalyst and doctor in clinical psychology and psychopathology, practicing in Paris and Lille. She is a co-founder of ALEPH (Association pour l'Étude de la Psychanalyse et de son Histoire), president of *Savoirs et clinique: association pour la formation en psychanalyse,* and adviser to the journal, *Savoirs et clinique* (Erès). She is also the author of numerous books and articles including: *Ambiguïtés sexuelles: sexuation et psychose* (Paris, Economica, 2000, also translated into Spanish); *L'Œuvre de Freud, l'invention de la psychoanalyse* (Paris, Bréal, 2006); *La Loi de la mère: essai sur le sinthome sexuel* (Paris, Economica, 2008, also translated into Spanish); *Clinique du suicide* (Toulouse, Erès, 2010); *Pantallas y suenos: ensayos psicoanaliticos sobre la imagen en movimiento* (Barcelona, ediciones S&P; 2011); *Sexual Ambiguities* (London, Karnac, 2011).

Leonardo Rodríguez is a psychoanalyst practicing in Melbourne, Australia. He is a founding member of the Australian Centre for Psychoanalysis; analyst member of l'École de Psychanalyse des Forums du Champ lacanien ; member of the Victorian Association of Psychoanalytic Psychotherapists; adjunct senior lecturer with the School of Psychiatry, Monash University; senior academic associate, School of Psychology and Social Science, Victoria University. He is also the author of *Psychoanalysis with Children: History, Theory and Practice* (London: Free Association Books, 1999) and numerous book chapters and articles on psychoanalytic theory and practice.

Colette Soler is a psychoanalyst practicing and teaching in Paris. She is a founder member of l'École de Psychanalyse des Forums du Champ lacanien, and has published numerous books and journal articles including: *What Lacan Said About Women* (Other Press, 2005); *L'inconscient à ciel ouvert de la psychose* (Presses Universitaires du Mirail, 2008); *Lacan: The Unconscious Reinvented* (Karnac, 2014); *Lacanian Affects: The Function of Affect in Lacan's Work* (Routledge, 2015).

Anne Worthington is a psychoanalyst and lecturer, based in London. She is a member of the Centre for Freudian Analysis and Research, The College of Psychoanalysts UK (where she is a member of board of governors) and the Guild of Psychotherapists (where she is on the training committee). She is also a lecturer at the Centre for Psychoanalysis, Middlesex University. Her publications include: "Freud's young female homosexual: a clinical exemplar of the Three Essays" (*Journal of the Centre for Freudian Analysis and Research*, 2008); and "Psychoanalysis and queer theory: as yet an 'unrealised promise'?" (in *Queer Sexualities: Staking Out New Territories in Queer Studies*, Oxford: Inter-disciplinary Press, 2012, of which she is the editor).

We have regularly used the plural "they" and "theirs", in place of "he" and "hers", in spite of the grammatical ungainliness, as we felt that the convention of opting for either masculine or feminine pronouns throughout would be inappropriate given the subject matter.

INTRODUCTION

Reclaiming hysteria

Anouchka Grose

Hysteria has proved one of the most popular and enduring diagnoses in medical history. Even before the fourth century BCE, when Hippocrates christened a cluster of "feminine" complaints under the title of "hysterikos" (of the womb) women were being treated for bad moods, seizures, and morbid thoughts—all of which were believed to be brought about by problems with the womb. The Kahun Gynaecological Papyrus (c.1900 BCE), the world's oldest known medical text, speaks about troubling movements of the organ inside the body. Later scripts describe coaxing the wayward flesh back into place using a combination of carefully placed, strong-smelling substances. (Nice smells near the vagina to draw the womb downwards, bad smells near the nose to make it retract, or vice versa.)

For thousands of years people have been alluding to women's physical and psychological complaints, trying to explain them and to come up with something to do about them. This "something" has veered from aromatherapy, to orgasm and childbirth, to exorcism—and then, in the late nineteenth century, to talking. The supposed causes have been equally inconstant, ranging from women's constitutional fragility, to sexual privation, original sin, demonological possession, and, finally, sociological factors. This last cause has the double-edged distinction of de-pathologising women, at the same time as moving the goalposts somewhat in terms of cure. From this standpoint, it's no longer the case that individual women need to be fixed (taking into account the fact that the unfortunate creatures are at a physiological or moral disadvantage) but that society as a whole needs to change, giving women more freedom and power.

In the first *Diagnostic and Statistical Manual of Mental Disorders (DSM-I)*, published in 1952, the American Psychiatric Association famously did away with the term "hysteria". It was apparently no longer useful, relevant, or even defensible. The British film, *Hysteria* (2011)—a gentle romcom about Victorians and vibrators—ends with this fact, presenting it as something of a victory, particularly for women. No longer would we be pathologised for being dissatisfied or unhappy. From now on things would be different. But how? Would we actually be any more satisfied? Or would our dissatisfactions simply continue to exist, but under different, better names?

In *DSM-I* you find the term "conversion reaction" where "hysteria" might have been. In spite of the lexical purge, physical symptoms with no known organic cause continue to be included, but any association with the wandering wombs of antiquity is out. Still, by the second edition, in 1968, hysteria had made its reappearance in the form of "hysterical neurosis (conversion type)". Then, from 1980 onwards it vanishes again, replaced by "conversion disorder", with "histrionic personality disorder" appearing elsewhere in the volume to describe—and slyly condemn—voluble, troubled women.

Before attempting to assess the usefulness of the term "hysteria" in current psychoanalytic practice we will go back and look more closely at the history of the diagnosis in order to see how it's changed. This is especially necessary in light of the often repeated idea that the sorts of clinical phenomena Freud and Breuer were seeing at the end of the nineteenth century are totally different from the kinds of things we're presented with today. According to many latter-day psychoanalytic commentators, in the olden days everyone was falling into hypnoid states and suffering various paralyses and contractures, while nowadays they suffer from eating disorders, panic attacks, shopaholism, or self-harm. By this account, you might form the idea that the roots of the illness are basically the same, only the symptoms are different.

All this is in turn complicated by the fact that, in the twenty-first century, we perhaps have a different idea of what psychoanalysis is for.

In the late nineteenth century people were largely being treated for all sorts of physically manifested symptoms, Freud's early work being to link their pains and seizures to unconscious ideas, rather than to look for organic causes. In contrast, people today almost exclusively turn up to analysis complaining of various types of unhappiness.

Behind all this, of course, lurks the question of the suppression of sexuality, and whether things are really any different in a society where everyone is supposedly allowed to let their sexuality follow whatever course it seems set on. There's no longer any need to sit around with your parents sewing and feeling frustrated. You can, in theory, go off and do whatever you like (including sewing). But does that make a difference to the kinds of symptoms people produce? And to the manner in which we might respond to them in an analytic setting?

From orgasm to exorcism and back

Hippocrates, circa 400 BCE, was an adherent of the ancient idea that the womb wandered around the body. According to archaic medicine, these travels resulted in the feminine complaints of nervousness, fluid retention, loss of appetite, and insomnia. Hippocrates believed that the trouble was caused by a blockage in the womb, or by the womb coming into contact with other organs. This would happen if a woman hadn't been having sex, meaning that her womb would dry out and become lighter, causing it to float around her body. Galen, over five hundred years later, also believed that hysteria was caused by an unsatisfactory sex life and pointed out that nuns, virgins, widows, and women with rotten husbands were particularly likely to suffer from it. He recommended pelvic massage by a midwife if other forms of sexual satisfaction proved unavailable. At the end of the first millennium the Islamic physician/philosopher/poet, Avicenna, repeated the notion that hysteria was caused by sexual dissatisfaction. He too had the idea that massage to orgasm was the cure, but that women shouldn't do it themselves. It had to be done either by their husbands or by a doctor, otherwise it would make them even worse.

So that was the good period, when people had vague, but still earthbound, ideas of what the causes of women's unhappiness might be—and largely humane ways of dealing with it. Then, in the Middle Ages, you have a disturbing phase when women's complaints—especially ones involving seizures and paralyses—are put down to their being inhabited by demons and they are subjected to exorcisms and/or being burnt at the stake. In the seventeenth century, thanks to the Enlightenment's dismissal of other-worldly explanations, the idea comes back that hysteria is caused by noxious gases in the womb. Doctors, searching for ideas untainted by superstition and religion, start to look back at Hippocrates, Galen, and Avicenna. This is when the word "hysterical" enters the English language, meaning an excess of feeling expressed by either laughter or tears.

By the nineteenth century it was still supposedly common practice for physicians to treat hysteria with pelvic massage or "vulvular stimulation" to the point of "hysterical paroxysm" (aka orgasm). In line with the Victorians' love of mechanisation they made things more efficient by using mechanical vibrators and hydrotherapy—jets of water directed at the clitoris. Although the cause of women's symptoms was thought to be sexual frustration, or difficulty with conception, the treatments were seen as purely functional—there was apparently nothing particularly awkward or embarrassing about them. Oddly enough, when the speculum was reintroduced into medical practice at the end of the nineteenth century—the Greeks and Romans had already used them—there was an outcry. People found it obscene, although they ostensibly accepted the fact that female hysteria could be treated by genital stimulation. (See Maines, 2001.)

Charcot and the psychogenic theory of hysteria

All of which perhaps gives us some idea of the world in which Jean-Martin Charcot was practising in the 1880s at the Salpetrière hospital in Paris. Charcot took the archaic diagnosis of hysteria and re-thought it in relation to the kinds of phenomena he was encountering at the hospital. He christened his new diagnosis "traumatic hysteria", thereby differentiating it from "female hysteria". Instead of being caused by the vagaries of the womb, the roots of the illness lay in traumatic events in the person's life (meaning that the sufferer might now be male). These traumas may also have involved physical injury, but Charcot was more interested in the psychic after-effects. He became curious about the ways in which thoughts and memories relating to the accident might unsettle the person in the present, causing anything from headaches to fits. The idea caught on rapidly, and soon any symptoms with no known organic causes were liable to be lumped into this category. Needless to say, in the late nineteenth century, there were plenty of medically perplexing symptoms.

Charcot's diagnostic imprecision has been a key starting point for attacks on his great follower, Freud. One of the most sustained and persuasive arguments against continued clinical use of the word "hysteria" is provided by Richard Webster in his book, *Why Freud was Wrong* (1995). After a rather dubious beginning (where Webster dismantles Freud's character using the most heavy-handed Freudian thinking—he was pushed to overreach by the unrealistically high expectations of his doting mother, apparently) he goes on to catalogue the many clinical errors made by Charcot, Freud, and their followers. Beginning with Charcot's celebrated work at the Salpêtrière, we see how the newly-theorised category of hysteria becomes a catch-all for any complaint without traceable organic origins. Instead of being realistic about their lack of knowledge, Charcot and his colleagues supposedly prefer to diagnose and treat their patients as if everything is under control. In this context, hysteria becomes an extremely useful diagnostic category because so many things can appear to be explained by it—and there are few, if any, means by which one can be proven wrong. This leads to a situation whereby people with brain tumours and lesions, concussion, and epilepsy regularly have their symptoms attributed to psychological trauma, are accordingly treated with hypnosis, and often die.

One can hardly blame nineteenth-century doctors for not possessing MRI scans and laser surgery. One can, however, accuse them of hubris, dogmatically diagnosing an "illness" with no demonstrable aetiology, and one which could be said to subtly put the patient in the wrong. As the story goes, these patients' symptoms weren't granted the dignity of an organic fact, but were attributed to psychological instability at best, malingering at worst. In either case the consequences could be fatal.

Charcot, in this account, is an unscrupulous self-publicist, using medicine to make himself rich and famous rather than to make people better. His shifting of the causes of hysteria away from the womb and on to the nervous system has the added benefit of meaning that male patients can now be misdiagnosed too. In his rabid pursuit of status, he turns the Salpêtrière into a circus, putting his flimsily dressed, excitingly convulsing ladies on show.

In Asti Hustvedt's book, *Medical Muses*, (2011) we hear about the overlap between the medical doctors and the stage hypnotists who circled around the hospital. While many of the doctors, including

Charcot, were apparently keen to distance themselves from the troublesome performers who threatened to bring the practice into disrepute, there were also those who moved between the two disciplines, all but abducting the hospital patients and taking them on degrading tours. On top of that there are accounts of stage hypnotists coming to the hospital as invited guests, presenting the secrets of their technique to the doctors.

As if all this wasn't confusing enough, Hustvedt also produces documents explaining how the patients performed for the doctors, competing for their attention with ever more extreme and picturesque manifestations of their "illness". Jane Avril, who later became a Moulin Rouge dancer, depicted in artworks by Toulouse Lautrec, was hospitalised during the early part of Charcot's reign. In her memoirs she speaks about the women at the hospital putting on florid and wholly fictitious displays "in order to capture attention and gain stardom".

So, you have doctors imposing a hokey diagnosis on as many patients as possible, and then certain of these patients compounding the situation, propping up the problematic diagnosis by perfectly enacting its symptomatology for the purposes of their own exhibitionism. Into this scene steps a twenty-nine-year-old Freud, keen to prove himself in the world of medicine (ostensibly in order to impress his mum). He witnesses Charcot's marvellous circumstances and covets them for himself. Absorbing what he can from this wildly flawed clinic he begins to extrapolate. Hence, according to the logic of Richard Webster, Freud could only ever have been wrong; setting out from such an erroneous starting point, he was lost before he began.

While Webster's hefty book provides painful reading for psychoanalytic sympathisers, it totally sidesteps the point of what actually goes on in a contemporary psychoanalytic clinic. It would be extremely rare for a psychoanalyst to be the first port of call for someone suffering from fits, paralyses, or any form of physical pain (the one exception being headaches, which are sometimes so easily traced to discomfiting events—visits from relatives, the presence of an exacting boss—as to be willingly self-diagnosed as psychogenic.) Although Freud's thinking might have its roots in nineteenth-century neurology, it also draws heavily on the subtleties of literature, a long tradition that doesn't require yet-to-be-invented technology to tell us that people act outside their best interests, suffer "inexplicably", and harbour irrational thoughts and feelings, of which they sometimes feel deeply ashamed.

To sum up, there's the longstanding idea that there is a particular kind of feminine malaise that has something to do with sex. Then there's a blip where you see something like a cultural psychosis; the link with sex becomes far more problematic (or foreclosed) and has to be represented by an idea such as demonic possession. Then the old idea is resuscitated and women are once again prescribed orgasms in the hope it will make them feel better. From here Charcot broadens the idea of hysteria to include all people who are suffering the after-effects of a trauma. Freud becomes interested and begins attempting to synthesise all the latest theories around hysteria, including those of Pierre Janet (dissociation theory) and Hippolyte Bernheim (treatment by hypnotic suggestion). He is also particularly enthralled by a treatment conducted by his older and more experienced friend, Joseph Breuer.

Anna O, again

The case of Anna O could be described as a fairy tale for psychoanalysts. It appears to bear endless retellings, but there's always the risk it might send you to sleep. Still, it needs to be wheeled on here to keep the thread running from the Kahun Papyrus to the contemporary clinic.

In November 1881, a little under four years before Freud's stint at Salpêtrière, Joseph Breuer began work with the patient he later called Anna O. She exhibited a bundle of distressing symptoms, including hypnoid states, contractures, trouble with vision, inadvertently speaking foreign languages, total loss of appetite, headaches, and hallucinations. A little way into Breuer's treatment of her she also apparently lost the power of speech. He happened to know, because he took an interest in his patients' lives, that she was offended about something and had decided not to talk about it. So he pushed her to tell him all about it, which she did, and then not only did she find herself able to speak again (albeit only in English) but she also regained the use of her left leg and hand. According to Breuer, "the psychical mechanism of the disorder became clear" (Breuer & Freud, 1893–95, p. 25). Anna's symptoms were ostensibly being caused by ideas or thoughts rather than by organic damage to the body or brain. Breuer's treatment of her came to centre on listening to her. It often appeared that if could make a link between a particular symptom of hers and the idea that had caused it, then the symptom would almost immediately vanish. In that sense, the case comes across as something like a miracle cure. Of course, we know now that this isn't the whole story and that it all ended in a big mess and freaked Breuer out so much that he no longer wanted anything to do with psychoanalysis, but that's not the impression you're left with at the end of the text itself. You have to read Ernest Jones's biography of Freud if you want to hear the other side of the story. In it Jones tells us that Breuer spoke about Anna O so incessantly that his wife became jealous and depressed. "It was a long time before Breuer, with his thoughts elsewhere, divined the meaning of [his wife's] state of mind. It provoked a violent reaction in him, perhaps compounded of love and guilt, and he decided to bring the treatment to an end" (Jones, 1953, p. 203). Anna was so shocked by his abrupt departure that she immediately relapsed, going into an alarming phantom labour. She spent the next few years in and out of hospital, with Breuer wishing her dead.

Freud, undeterred by the explosiveness of Breuer's treatment, decided to further explore the possibilities of the "talking cure". His idea at the time was to take Charcot's idea of the hidden psychical trauma behind a symptom and to link it with Breuer's cathartic method. In 1889 he went to work very seriously on a case of hysteria, the first one he had tried to treat using these new ideas and methods. With his patient, Emmy von N, he used hypnosis and suggestion, as well as trying to get her to link her symptoms to unsettling events in her past. (She also underwent massage and hydrotherapy. We don't have precise details of the forms this took, although readers of Rachel P. Maine's book might be inclined to speculate …) Emmy von N hallucinates, has facial tics and certain phrases that she repeatedly shouts, as well as making what Freud calls "a curious clacking" sound with her mouth. Following Charcot, he keeps asking about things that have given her a fright. She seems to have had lots of frights in her life and produces tons of memories. Her siblings threw dead animals at her, she thought she saw a kind of apparition sitting up in bed, her husband dropped dead in front of her, she saw a big lizard on stage, creepy men appeared in her bedroom, and so it goes on. The case doesn't appear quite as magical as Anna O's, but Emmy von N does nonetheless lose the odd symptom. The treatment is peculiar in that, a lot of the time, Freud tells her to remember things under hypnosis, and then immediately tells her to forget them. This forgetting of upsetting events is clearly effective at some level because she tells him later that she seems to be missing large chunks of memory.

To return to the idea of hysteria today, you can see that these early cases don't necessarily present us with symptoms that no longer exist. One might very well come across people who clack and hallucinate and fall into trances, but we would be unlikely to diagnose hysteria in those cases. Twenty-first-century doctors would be far more likely to find epilepsy, Tourette's, concussion, aphasia caused by brain lesions, etc., and modern psychoanalysts would also be unlikely to expect those sorts of symptoms to clear up with a bit of talking. If you take on patients like that, you'd better not put them off the idea of going to see a medical doctor. However, if they do come your way—perhaps after a series of fruitless medical examinations—an analyst faced with a contemporary Anna O or an Emmy von N would be likely to consider the possibility of psychosis. The symptoms are so extreme—the hallucinations, the trances, that degree of somatisation—that you might suspect you're not looking at someone slightly repressed, but at a person with very serious pathologies and some pretty ferocious defence mechanisms.

So, not only was the treatment of those cases very different—hydrotherapy, hypnosis, suggestion, massage—all things we certainly wouldn't do ourselves as psychoanalysts these days (although plenty of people outside the psychoanalytic clinic still do) but also the diagnosis of hysteria was made far more broadly and readily than one would make it today. So you can see this isn't the same as saying that the symptoms of hysteria have changed due to cultural conditions favouring different choices of symptom. It's not simply that people used to go into trances and lose the use of their limbs and now they starve and cut themselves. People clearly do both things now, and did both then (which isn't to say that cultural conditions don't play their part, but that's another discussion. See Darian Leader, below). It's more that those diagnoses were made at a very particular time in history and now those people's illnesses would almost certainly be understood another way. Or in a number of other ways, because there's not all that much agreement about it, either within the psychoanalytic world, or outside it.

If that's the case, then what can we possibly hope to learn from those studies? Or from the theory around those cases? Are they just of historical interest? A charming soporific? Or are there things in them that are still relevant to clinical practice?

Freud and Breuer's theories were very much in progress in the late 1890s. Maybe because of that there is an incredible clarity in some of the writing. For instance, in Breuer's section on "Unconscious ideas and ideas inadmissible to consciousness—splitting of the mind" (Breuer & Freud, 1993–95, p. 222) you get a really brilliant and precise description of the way in which unconscious ideas might influence our daily lives. Breuer describes a business man who has been annoyed by something in the morning and then goes to work and immerses himself in his business so that his conscious thoughts are totally taken up with whatever it is he's doing. He doesn't think at all about this thing that annoyed him, but all his decisions are influenced by it and he says "no" to things he might otherwise have said "yes" to. So Breuer argues for the existence of ideas that are operative "beneath the threshold of consciousness" in our lives, a few years before Freud wrote *The Psychopathology of Everyday Life* (1901). Although it has become one of the most well-known ideas associated with psychoanalysis, it's still something that people in and out of analysis might find hard to accept. You regularly hear people say things like, "I was very upset about it at the time, but I don't see how it relates to what I'm going through now." Or, "Do you really think that might have something to do with this?" And while we might no longer have the hope that if people can link their current difficulties to events in their past they might immediately find themselves happy and well, we are still obviously going to be looking for the ways in which people's histories, or even prehistories (stories about their grandparents, etc.) are operative in the present in ways of which they might be consciously unaware.

As for the early psychoanalytic cases themselves, and how they might be useful, Breuer has something to say about it early on in his text on Anna O. He tells us that although her type of illness is common enough and not particularly fascinating in itself, the thing that makes it interesting is its intelligibility. Anna discusses events and ideas in a way that seems to have a direct impact on her symptoms. And she has lots of ideas about how her symptoms got there in the first place. Breuer likens it to the way in which a sea urchin's eggs are encased in a transparent membrane, meaning that we can actually watch the embryo develop. Because of this, sea urchins are important to embryologists in spite of not being (according to Breuer) particularly interesting. Anna is worthy of study because she likes to reveal her thoughts, and these thoughts appear to Breuer to be the very thing out of which her illness is built. As he very touchingly puts it, "her life became known to me to an extent to which one person's life is seldom known to another." Less touchingly, he runs off as soon as he realises it's serious, leaving it to Freud to develop a proper theory of transference. Breuer seems a bit naive, or repressed, where Anna's sexuality is concerned and, as soon as it emerges, he can't take it. But before that happens she certainly teaches him a thing or two about how an idea can inform a symptom—albeit in a strange, rather concrete way that kind of skims along the surface and doesn't involve itself explicitly with the disturbing business of sexuality. His idea about Anna's sea urchinness has a kind of charming wrongness about it, as if her speech actually renders her psyche visible. It doesn't appear to occur to him at all that she may be doing something with him by speaking, rather than simply revealing her inner workings in an unproblematic way. It's surely obvious to any careful reader, from the very beginning of the case, that this is going to be a love story, and that this whole business of speaking and revealing and listening and responding isn't at all the same process as an embryologist tracking changes in a see-through egg. (It isn't hard to imagine, though, that embryologists can get very attached to the creatures they are studying, and perhaps Breuer's brusque and unreasonable dismissal of sea urchins tells us everything we need to know about his disavowed feelings for Anna. I only hope his wife didn't read the essay.)

In Freud's early cases he picks up the thread of the ideogenic nature of hysterical symptoms, but gives far more weight than Breuer to the sexual material that emerges in his patients' discourse, and to the feelings and ideas the patient might have about him. It's funny that, because of this, people sometimes suggest that Freud pretty much discovered sex, or at least saw it everywhere, when it's clear that the link between hysterical symptoms and love and sex had already been apparent for at least four millennia. Freud's innovation was to try to be more precise about what those connections might be and how they might work, and also to treat his patients using words, rather than physical interventions, which were basically replacements for the sexual act, or sexual acts under a different banner. You might even argue that Freud made hysteria less sexy.

Modern love

Many of the social advancements suggested by feminist writers and activists, from Mary Wollstonecraft to Gloria Steinem, have now come to pass. Women in Western democracies can vote, divorce, have sex for pleasure, earn money, wear trousers, and express opinions without necessarily expecting to be patronised. Of course hysteria is no longer listed in the *DSM*! What on earth would we need an "illness" like that for? We no longer have to express dissatisfaction and desire through questionable, non-organic symptoms. In this new world, a diagnosis of hysteria could surely only be a terrible affront, harking back to a situation where women had so little agency that the only way they could claw back a bit of control was to use illness as a form of resistance. We don't need to do that anymore, do we?

In Helene Deutsch's *Neuroses and Character Types* (1965) she begins with a chapter (first published in 1930) about the place of the "actual conflict" in the formation of a neurotic illness. By "actual conflict" she means the present life circumstances which make an illness necessary. She takes the cases of three women, each of whom has fallen in love with a man who isn't her husband. According to Deutsch, the choice these women faced was whether to let themselves have an affair, to renounce the affair and look for some other form of satisfaction, or to succumb to a neurotic illness. They all chose the latter, hence their appearance in Deutsch's office. She then follows the courses of three very different sets of symptoms produced out of the same initial problem.

This question of whether to follow an erotic impulse or not is also important for Freud, and in psychoanalytic literature in general. It hardly needs pointing out that it can cause quite a few problems if a clinician gets it into his or her head that the necessary solution to a person's difficulties is to go ahead and act on impulse. When, in the Dora case, Freud decides that Dora's problem is that she can't admit to herself that she is in love with Herr K, she gives up on him and his treatment. In Dora's case it's even more extreme because she's never actually said she fancies Herr K; Freud just decides she must be in love with him and that if she could only admit it to herself it would help her. In "'Civilised' sexual morality and modern nervous illness" (1908), Freud proposes that people's restrictive ideas about sexuality are an exacerbating factor in the production of illnesses; if people could stop being so stuffy they might also stop feeling so awful. It's a very nice, liberal argument but, while you probably don't want to argue in favour of bringing back Victorian sexual standards, it seems not to be true that greater sexual freedom necessarily results in greater happiness. Of course, Freud understood this perfectly well, and essays such as "*Beyond the Pleasure Principle*" (1920) have plenty to say about it. Following on from here, Lacan really takes up all of that and shows the ways in which prohibitions may be extremely helpful to people; they obscure the real issue, which is that unproblematic enjoyment is pretty much out of the question.

One wouldn't have to search hard to find a contemporary case where all sorts of problems are produced out of the same "actual conflict" as the one faced by Helene Deutsch's patients. A woman who is living with her partner suddenly finds herself overwhelmed by strong feelings for someone else. That she and her boyfriend are not married, plus the fact that the house is wholly in her name, doesn't do anything to reduce the anxiety around the choice she finds herself having to make. She suggests they try having an open relationship, which is obviously a very modern solution, but the man declines and immediately moves in with another woman. The first woman is totally shocked and all sorts of very unsettling feelings follow. The fact that there is no enormous social stigma attaching to a separation, and that open relationships are supposedly available as a great solution to the problem of long-term monogamy, does little to help her; she still falls into a terrible state, feels unable to work or see friends, and urgently seeks treatment.

If hysteria can be loosely characterised as a neurotic illness with a psychosexual cause, then contemporary people are no nearer to solving the problems of sexuality than people at any other time. It's still something totally perplexing. The obstacles to enjoyment aren't simply external things such as social disapproval, but are more structural and intrinsic to the formation of sexuality itself. If you are allowed to do whatever you like, that doesn't mean you will actually like it, and neurotic subjects develop their own ways of coming at that fact. It seems that the task of psychoanalysis has been, and carries on being, to try to come up with adequate ways to understand and respond to the suffering that comes out of that.

New words for old problems

So where does that leave the tainted diagnosis of hysteria? Why would psychoanalysts retain an attachment to such a famously problematic word? Since Charcot's rethinking of the causes of the disease, the word is no longer etymologically appropriate, and the rethinking itself has also been thrown into deep suspicion. If psychoanalysis wants to keep its place in contemporary discourse it should surely distance itself from such a troublesome history.

But if "hysteria" is out, what comes in its place? There are various ways in which to attempt to answer this question. One is to say that hysteria was only ever an approximate and erroneous idea that used a basic misapprehension to "explain" a plethora of phenomena. Now it's gone, we can get on with attempting proper medical diagnoses. Another possibility—opened up by Freud, and developed further by Lacan—is to interpret the troublesome, malleable complaints offered up by certain people as a mode of address to the Other. Before rushing to state that this is plainly the best option, it might be useful to look at the alternative.

What constitutes a "proper" medical diagnosis? On the one hand it might mean something like spotting a growth or a lesion, and treating it with appropriate drugs or surgery. This is a great way to come at the problem, but it does rely on there being an organic disease in the first place. When people turn up to neurology clinics, this is very often not the case. You're still regularly left with the problem of what to do next. It may be that they have an organic problem that has yet to be recognised by medicine. If you believe this is so, there's very little you can do—except to send them to a counsellor to help them deal with the miserable notion of having an unknown, but definitely bona fide, physical complaint, meanwhile telling them to keep an eye on the Internet for proper scientific updates. (Lucky counsellor!)

Alternatively, perhaps they are manifesting an inarticulable psychological complaint, in which case you're back in Charcot-land. Still, if you accept the idea that their complaint may be psychologically underpinned, you may want them to be properly medically diagnosed by a psychiatrist using reliable modern methods (otherwise known as checklists). Perhaps they have a personality disorder or Munchausen syndrome. A visit to a psychiatrist will help to establish whether they are "too" this or "too" that, to pinpoint their maladaptive behaviours and deviations. In other words, they will be measured against the psychiatrist's highly scientific notion of "normality" and either found wanting or not. If they are chemically depressed or genetically delusional they may be offered drugs, but if they're just "not quite right" they may be sent to a therapist whose brief, cheap, empirically testable form of treatment will help them to adapt their being to a more standard model. This will be done by telling the patient what they're getting wrong, and encouraging them to correct it, perhaps using carefully placed Post-it notes as an aide-mémoire—one on the credit card, another on the razor blades, or wherever seems most pertinent.

While this might sound like a rather glib parody of the state of contemporary mental healthcare, it will also be familiar to anyone practicing in the psychodynamic tradition. Our offices are full of people who've passed through the medical system and found it wanting. They know perfectly well that the "cure" for anorexia is eating, and that shopaholism can, in theory, be controlled by a sensible cash flow chart, stringently adhered to. This knowledge does little to help them. They come to analysis to try to know something about the mismatch between knowledge and desire, or sense and nonsense. They may start out by trying to understand, for instance, how their relationship with their parents or their siblings underpins their particular form of suffering, but gradually realise that the stories they construct to explain themselves to themselves can only go a certain way towards making them feel better. Beyond their wish to make sense of something lies the realisation that sense can't cover everything, or that one's existence can't be sewn up with words. By tolerating paradoxes, exploring conflicting tendencies, and being aware of inconsistencies in their own discourse, they might eventually open up the possibility of a less fraught relationship with the cracks in their being.

In the 1970s Lacan (1969–70) began to talk about "hystericising" the analysand, meaning opening them up to questions and incongruities. As opposed to persuading troublesome people to be more sensible, we're invited to consider the alternative, of allowing semi-sensible people to become more unhinged. This would be necessary in the case of obsessional patients, who might otherwise remain stuck in a state of battened-down psychic rigidity. Far from portraying hysterics as people who foolishly manufacture symptoms in a doomed attempt to buck the system, they are here seen as people who refuse easy answers, resisting commonplace idiocies put forward in the form of accepted laws and norms. They use their dissatisfactions and discomforts as a means to interrogate the Other, to make it say something back, to attempt to unsettle it. In this sense the hysteric can be seen as a seeker after truth. It may seem a counter-intuitive leap from the idea of the Victorian malingerer, but the two could be said to be in direct relation. By virtue of their very unhappiness, hysterics have always found ways to attack the status quo. "Illness" offers a form of resistance.

In his four discourses—Lacan's response to the upheavals of 1968—he sets up the hysteric's discourse as precisely that which can overturn fixity and uncover new lines of inquiry (in spite of famously telling the students-in-revolt, "You demand a new master. You will get one!"). He puts the hysteric on the side of science—not the obsessional notion of science that refuses to entertain an idea until it has been thoroughly tamed by proof, but the investigative, relentless, fluctuating possibilities of a science that never accepts any answer as final and remains forever open to the likelihood of being wrong.

It is in this sense that we can speak about "hysteria today" without being frightened off by the dual spectres of bad medicine and defunct gender definitions. At least in the Lacanian clinic, a diagnosis of hysteria is anything but an affront. Dissatisfaction is the motor for desire, and desire drives existence. Hysterics specialise at using dissatisfaction to keep desire spinning, acting against atrophy and ossification. Far from trying to get them to stop fussing and get back in line, one might encourage them to take their questioning further, to use it in their lives and work, and even to attempt to enjoy it.

This book is a collection of essays showing a number of ways in which one might think productively around the idea of hysteria in the contemporary clinic. It doesn't disavow the troublesome backstory of the word, but keeps it in mind while trying to consider the implications of a condition that changes its form to suit its circumstances and never lets itself be explained out of existence.

References

Breuer, J., & Freud, S. (1893–95). *Studies on Hysteria. S. E., 2*. London: Hogarth.
Deutsch, H. (1965). *Neuroses and Character Types: Clinical Psychoanalytic Studies*. Madison, CT: International Universities Press.
Didi-Huberman, G. (1982). *Invention of Hysteria: Charcot and the Photographic Iconography of the Salpêtrière*. London: MIT Press, 2004.
Freud, S. (1901). *The Psychopathology of Everyday Life. S. E., 6*. London: Hogarth.
Freud, S. (1908). "Civilised" sexual morality and modern nervous illness. *S. E., 9*. London: Hogarth.
Freud, S. (1920). *Beyond the Pleasure Principal. S. E., 8*. London: Hogarth.
Hustvedt, A. (2011). *Medical Muses: Hysteria in Nineteenth-Century Paris*. London: Norton.

Jones, E. (1953). *The Life and Work of Sigmund Freud.* London: Hogarth, 1962.
Lacan, J. (1969–70). *The Seminar of Jacques Lacan: The Other Side of Psychoanalysis: Vol. XVII.* London: Norton, 2007.
Maines, R. P. (2001). *The Technology of Orgasm: "Hysteria," the Vibrator, and Women's Sexual Satisfaction.* Baltimore, MD: Johns Hopkins University Press.
Webster, R. (1995). *Why Freud Was Wrong: Sin, Science and Psychoanalysis.* London: Fontana, 1996.

CHAPTER ONE

Hysterics today

Leonardo S. Rodríguez

A long history

Hysteria and hysterics have occupied physicians, philosophers, playwrights, and poets since antiquity. They have been a key presence in the history of psychoanalysis since its inception, and Freud credited a hysterical patient with having made a substantial contribution to the creation of the psychoanalytic method, when this was only in its gestational phase (Freud, 1895d, p. 56). Yet, having adopted them since the nineteenth century, the psychiatry of our times tends to avoid the use of the terms "hysteria" and "hysterics", and prefers other nomenclatures to designate clinical phenomena that, from a psychoanalytic perspective, are typically hysterical. The last edition of the *Diagnostic and Statistical Manual of Mental Disorders* does not even mention hysteria, while the psychoanalyst will recognise hysterical phenomena (even if not exclusively) throughout that text under a diversity of headings: "Anxiety disorders"; "Dissociative disorders"; "Somatic symptom and related disorders"; "Sexual dysfunctions"; and probably under other categories (American Psychiatric Association, 2013).

The terms currently used in psychiatric nomenclature to refer to hysterical phenomena are less precise than the psychoanalytic usage of "hysteria", "hysterics", "conversion hysteria", and "anxiety hysteria": in the psychoanalytic practice informed by the works of Sigmund Freud and Jacques Lacan an effort is made to distinguish real hysterical symptoms from symptoms and signs that may resemble hysteria but which do not belong to the same clinical category.

There is a certain irony in referring to "symptoms and signs that may resemble hysteria" but which do not belong in hysteria "proper". Until Freud, hysterical phenomena of the conversion type "resembled" physical symptoms and signs, accepted as "genuine" by a medicine oriented by the knowledge and clinical principles available at the time. But the resemblance to "true" symptoms and signs engendered the suspicion that hysterical phenomena could not be regarded as serious matters for scientific research and clinical practice. They were considered imitations, simulations of true disease, artefacts aimed at generating sympathy, at saving the sufferer from work on the grounds of sickness, at being spared from the duties and exigencies of human life: cases of fraudulent individuals, even if it was recognised that the conscious intentions of these individuals might not be deliberately deceitful, and that they might have justifiable motives to pose as ill people—disappointments in life or tragic circumstances that rendered their attempts at peculiar forms of fraud forgivable.

The words "hysteria" and "hysteric" have nevertheless survived outside psychiatric circles, in ordinary usage. They continue to be popular in English (as do equivalent terms in other languages), although they tend to be employed in a pejorative sense: "She became hysterical", "These people have developed mass hysteria", etc.

In psychoanalysis of the Lacanian orientation (which has always maintained its Freudian foundations), hysteria and hysterics continue to be the appropriate terms for well-established concepts that operate as clear reference-points in clinical practice. Hysteria designates different forms of neurosis—a plurality of typical neurotic formations that constitute variations of the same clinical structure—with a degree of clarity and specificity that contrast with the diffuse meanings assigned to the terms that have replaced it in the discourse of psychiatry. Furthermore, beyond what Freud first envisaged in his clinical practice and research, hysteric has become the denomination (particularly in the works of Lacan and the psychoanalysts inspired by Lacan) for first, a modality of discourse that is fundamental in the constitution of bonds between human beings, and second, an essential dimension of the complex relations that humans maintain with their own bodies, in so far as these bodies are not treated as purely natural entities but are always approached through the mediation of linguistic and cultural artefacts. This extension of the concept does not affect the precision that is required in a clinical practice: on the contrary, it has thrown further light upon hysterical clinical presentations and our orientation in their treatment—in particular, the diverse modalities in the development of the transference-relation by patients in analysis, the strategy for the handling of the transference on the part of the analyst, and the somatic manifestations of the workings of the unconscious.

The etymology of the words hysteria and hysteric illustrates the intimate links that exist between discourse, the human body, and hysterical phenomena. For a long time it was believed that these words, whose usage became frequent in medical and other circles from the sixteenth century, derived from the Greek *uterós*, "uterus", and some passages of Plato's *Timaeus* were interpreted as involving a pre-scientific theory of conversion hysteria, according to which the typical symptoms of this disturbance, already recognised by the Greeks of the classical period, would emanate from the activity (or hyperactivity, rather) of a "wandering womb", itself propelled to travel in an unusual way to different locations of the internal body by a state of sexual dissatisfaction (Plato, 1961, pp. 1194, 1195, 1199, 1210). A study by M. J. Adair published years ago contests that interpretation, and argues that it is based on an incorrect translation of the original terms employed by Plato, which should be better rendered as "wandering desire" rather than "wandering uterus" or "womb" (Adair, 1997).

Not being a Greek scholar, I am not in a position to judge on the validity of Adair's interpretation. If this author were right, Plato's theory, without having any "solid" scientific or clinical foundation, would still be closer to the psychoanalytic findings concerning conversion hysteria than the interpretation based on a fictional account of the life of an unhappy uterus. At any rate, it is interesting to note that the two alternative interpretations of Plato's text are based on the intuitive assumption that the mechanism of symptom-formation in conversion hysteria involves either a displacement of an organ (albeit an anatomical displacement, rather than a symbolic one) or the transposition of a mental formation on to bodily manifestations, as well as a sexual aetiology, that is, a state of lack of satisfaction of either a circumscribed sexual organ or the entire sexual desiring subject.

If hysteria has retained a prominent place in our lives and culture despite the disavowal to which it has been subjected by contemporary psychiatry, this is because it concerns the foundations of human existence, that is to say, language and the body: spoken words and their impact upon our corporeal habitat, in which, and through which, we create and destroy bonds with one another, we love and hate, we suffer and rejoice.

After Freud

A few lines of Freud's "Comparative study" of 1893 condenses what was already known in medical circles about hysteria of the conversion type, as Freud would later call it:

> [...] *in its paralyses and other manifestations hysteria behaves as though anatomy did not exist or as though it had no knowledge of it* [...] It takes the organs in the ordinary, popular sense of the names they bear: the leg is the leg as far up as its insertion into the hip, the arm is the upper limb as it is visible under the clothing. (Freud, 1893c, p. 169)

It demanded nothing less than the clinical and epistemic revolution that Freud brought to this world to explain this strange state of affairs.

Grounded on a clinical experience rich in questions and enigmas for someone more interested in what was not known than in applying established knowledge therapeutically, Freud articulated a theory of conversion hysteria (Freud, 1894a, p. 49) and, fifteen years later, of anxiety hysteria (Freud, 1909b). Freud's fertile clinical and theoretical production during the last decade of the nineteenth century enabled him to identify a formative, structural, and structuring link between hysterical symptoms, the modalities through which hysterical patients typically address the Other verbally, the constitutive mechanisms of the unconscious and its formations (dreams, parapraxes, jokes), and the method of free association, which has served analysands and analysts so well over the past 120 years.

It is highly improbable that the secret of the hysterical symptom could have seen the light of day outside the new discourse created by Freud, of which the method of free association is an instrument. No "objective" procedure that attempts to by-pass the patient's subjectivity has been efficient in uncovering the causes of hysterical symptoms.

"Subjectivity" is here used in a non-speculative sense: it refers to that which in the human subject remains largely unknown yet partially manifest in traces materialised by words and silences, in dreams, in peculiar expressions of the unconscious that are expressed through the body (conversion symptoms and anxiety), and in the eccentricity of obsessive ideas and compulsive acts. The method of free association created by Freud enables the analysand's unconscious subjectivity to be revealed systematically in a way that no other human discourse has been able to achieve: poetry, the arts, and the different forms of neurotic and psychotic madness also reveal the unconscious, but they do not so systematically, and when they do the revelation is cryptic, enigmatic, and requires interpretation—the interpretation for which psychoanalysis has provided a rationale and a practical guide. The Freudian method has made it possible to develop an efficient therapeutic approach to the neuroses, the psychoses, and the perversions based on the respect for, and analysis of, subjectivity.

The essential attributes and components of human subjectivity today remain as they were in Freud's times, in the same way as the structures of language and the human body have not changed essentially—the comparison is not accidental, as there is a correspondence between subjectivity, language, and the body, even if they belong in different levels of organisation.

What have changed, however, are the ways in which the dominant discourses define, approach, and materially deal with our subjectivity, and consequently the ways in which we, as individual subjects—subjects *subjected to* these discourses—deal with it. In this connection, the reference to capitalist discourse, and the ideals represented by forms of jouissance promoted by a society of consumers, has become commonplace. This reference is not incorrect, but it is insufficient to explain the contemporary modalities of human subjectivity. We have become used to hearing that the human subject has been practically abolished and has become a senseless consumer, an automaton dominated by the pursuit of useless and self-destructive forms of jouissance. Although recognising the bit of truth contained in such statements, one must nevertheless pay attention to the multiple manifestations of human subjectivity still present in the life of the arts and the sciences, in social and political movements, and in what touches us directly—neurotics and psychoanalysis. The reduction of human subjects to consumers does not result in the elimination of subjectivity: the capitalist mode of production, and its apparatuses of publicity and propaganda, still depend upon the generation of choices that, although forced and narrow, require nevertheless the enactment of subjectivity. This is not less a subjectivity for being the subjectivity of our troubled times.

The capitalist discourse and its scientific and technological supports were already dominant in Freud's cultural milieu (cf. his *Civilization and its Discontents*, Freud, 1930a). The material and ideological conditions determined by capitalism, science, and technology in Western societies in the nineteenth century promoted the creation of psychoanalysis by a single man who, for ten years, worked, as he put it, "in splendid isolation". The same conditions simultaneously favoured the resistances against psychoanalysis (cf. Freud's "A difficulty in the path of psychoanalysis", 1917a): this is only one among other instances of the contradictions that emerge in a dynamic culture.

If psychoanalysis has survived the many difficulties it has encountered in its path, this is because of the good work of a few psychoanalysts, but also because of the good work of neurotics (and psychotics, and perverts), whose psychopathology has served as a refuge for their subjectivity. Some of them have embarked on a psychoanalysis, thus choosing to learn something from their own psychopathology and perhaps move beyond it. For that purpose they have had to struggle against their own resistances, as well as cultural resistances. Yet these resistances are a function of the unconscious, and one can learn from them and eventually create something out of them—something modest that may well remain unnoticed, or alternatively something that represents a tangible social contribution, from the ordinary tasks of everyday life to artistic or scientific sublimations. Hysterics, too, contribute to our culture in better ways than the stereotypical figure of the histrionic and forever whining creature.

It was Freud who first linked hysteria and subjectivity in practice, and not only in theory, by listening to the hysteric *qua* subject and learning about hysteria from that subject—rather than attempting to deal with hysteria as an object-illness, a de-subjectified entity that could be examined as an infectious disease, a malignant tumour, or a metabolic disorder.

What is new, if anything, in the hysterics of today? Are they relatives of those that Freud treated in the last years of the nineteenth century?

Apart from the psychiatrists and other professionals who regard hysteria as something of the past, or who simply foreclose its existence, there are people (including many psychoanalysts) who believe that hysteria and hysterics do exist; yet they also believe that today's hysterics are very different from Freud's patients in their clinical presentation, presumably because the cultural conditions under which the hysterics of today have grown (and in particular the social habits and regulations concerning sexuality) have changed radically over the last century. From this perspective, we could still recognise the existence of hysteria as a clinical structure, but its typical symptoms would differ markedly from those presented by Elisabeth von R. and the other patients that Freud inscribed in history by making them the central characters in the pieces of the new genre that he created: the psychoanalytic case history.

This new genre, and the style of Freud's presentation of his hysterical patients, have been as decisive as his more theoretical works in our comprehension and the clinical efficacy that we have been able to obtain in the treatment of contemporary patients. Freud's case histories constitute substantial components of the conceptual corpus of psychoanalysis and have moulded what generations of psychoanalysts have regarded as "a case": the narrative of the real vicissitudes of the singular psychoanalytic treatment of a unique patient by an equally unique analyst. They are vivid accounts of the discourse that Freud created, one in which the "case" (etymologically: "fall", "chance", "occurrence", i.e., that which falls within a category) *spoke* to someone who *listened*—and who listened because he was interested in what the hysteric had to say, the way in which she said it, and her peculiar style of addressing the interlocutor.

None of the clinical *facts* of hysteria, or for that matter of any neurosis, psychosis, perversion, or other "case" hard to assign to any of the established nosological categories, would exist had Freud not invented that new form of talking and engaging with other human beings—the psychoanalytic clinical experience—which since Lacan we call *the psychoanalytic discourse*.

In its essence this discourse, if applied according to the rationale that Freud established for it a hundred or more years ago, has not changed to this day (Freud, 1895d, 1900a, 1905e, 1912b, 1912e, 1913c, 1914g, 1915a). This is a remarkable fact, as during the same period an extraordinary number of works published by psychoanalysts in several languages provide testimonies of the most diverse conceptual and clinical orientations within the psychoanalytic movement. Despite this diversity, all the analysts who identify with a Freudian affiliation share the same fundamental principles and rules in conducting their clinical practices, even if they explain and justify their experience and actions in very different terms.

The hysterics of today are not *that* different from those who lived in Vienna in the 1890s, and that is why we continue to employ the word. They are different because everybody today is different from the Viennese of those days (including the Viennese of today) in a number of significant ways: culturally, socially, linguistically, even physiologically and biochemically, if one takes into account advances in the sciences and practices concerned with human health, as well as the modern diets and the various regimes aimed at preserving the integrity of muscles and bones which hold our bodies together. The Viennese of the end of the nineteenth century, hysterical or otherwise, were different in significant ways from their contemporaries living in other places, languages, and cultures, in the same way as we are very different from our contemporaries in other continents and/or cultural environments. As the capital of the Austro-Hungarian Empire, a melting pot of different ethnic groups, the population of Vienna itself was not uniform, but very diverse: Freud's biography is a testimony of this.

Freud's first major discovery in the clinic of hysteria is the mechanism of formation of the conversion symptom. This mechanism has not changed in its structure. What Freud described as typical conversion symptoms continue to be prevalent, even if there are now variations that derive from new social practices, such as the widespread use of medically prescribed and illegal drugs and the supposedly more "liberated" forms of sexuality, as well as the changes in linguistic usage, which provides material verbal support for the bodily organs and functions affected by symptoms. The psychoanalyst of today must remain attentive to variations in the interpretation of expressive bodily phenomena within the populations of our cosmopolitan cities (London, Paris, New York, Melbourne, and others), as the conversion symptoms of today reflect in their "formal" presentation the diversity of linguistic backgrounds and social customs of our patients.

Before coining new meanings for the terms that constitute the core of psychoanalytic vocabulary—"unconscious", "repression", "conversion", "obsessional neurosis", "defence"—and before the inaugural dream that decided his fate as creator of psychoanalysis (the dream of "Irma's injection"; Freud, 1900a), Freud already knew that in its formation the conversion symptom is co-determined by the linguistic usage of common words, themselves grounded in the sociocultural practices of a community. As mentioned earlier, it was known before Freud that hysteria "interprets" organs of the body and their functions in the popular, non-scientific sense of the words that ordinary discourse attaches to them, and it uses those words and their bodily representations to express a dramatic conflict kept under the secrecy of repression.

Freud was able to decipher the bodily expressions of repressed words and phrases, thus uncovering an order of unconscious causality—grounded in unconscious inscriptions (*Niederschriften*) and mechanisms—that defies and alters the natural anatomic and physiological organisation of the living organism. The repressed words and phrases are structured and determined by a human-made organisation, the order of language itself, which has a formative effect upon the three registers of the human subject's experience, designated by Jacques Lacan as the symbolic, the imaginary, and the real. Those words and phrases, arranged according to the phonological, grammatical, and pragmatic rules of language, impose their marks upon the subject through the contingent yet decisive episodes of actual discourse that make his/her unconscious history—spoken words, verbal expressions of love and hate, of praise and admonition, commands, demands, supplications.

A patient of mine suffered from a rather severe form of *astasia abasia*, which as a symptom had occupied a central position in her history. At some crucial moments in her life she felt that she was going to fall to the ground, so that she needed the physical support of someone else. She would then hold on to the other person's hand, shoulder, or any part of the other's body she could reach. She would hold on to the shoulders of her young children when going out with them, despite their not being able to provide solid material support. She would hold on to my hands as I opened the door when she arrived for her session. She also spoke of "holding on to" when seeking advice from other people, which she did repeatedly, usually over the telephone, as at times she felt incapable of taking any decisions, ranging from the very serious to the most trivial.

The analysis revealed that she was unconsciously fixated upon a sentence of her mother's. When the patient was a young child, her mother declared to her, using an expression in a language other than English: "You shall always need a crutch!" The word in her original language, translated here as "crutch", has approximately the same meaning as in English (although it is not used in the sense of "crotch", as in English). In the patient's view, her mother herself had never offered to be her crutch or given her any support when she felt she needed it. So, she persevered through her symptom in making sure she obeyed the mother's rule. Ostensibly she had been very disobedient to her mother in every other aspect of her life; but the real dimension of the unconscious dominating her symptoms and significant acts was in fact docile towards the fascinating power of a tyrannical mother, combined with the interpretation of her father as a weak creature, more submissive to the mother than herself.

Another analysand, a young girl of four, developed severe constipation that required admission to hospital, where she was given enemas and received other medical interventions. She was brought to me after her discharge and told me her story. She had gone to hospital "to have a baby", she said. It had happened, and now she was happy, she added. We worked out that she had identified with her best friend's mother, who had had a baby not long before, after a pregnancy that had been surrounded by mysterious evasions of her questions regarding the lady's tummy, and uncertainty about the reasons for her young friend's bad mood and scenes of jealousy. The faeces in her tummy became her baby, a metaphorical use of the body I have observed in other young girls who presented with symptoms of constipation and encopresis.

Given our exposure to discourse and its impositions, and given the plasticity of the human body, which makes it possible to dramatically stage intentions and actions, conflicts and unwanted desires, the human capacity for hysterisation of bodily functions is virtually universal—the exception being the autistic subject, for whom the equivocality of the signifier is excluded: the equivocality that makes possible the transposition of a verbal command, "You shall always need a crutch", or the verbal expression of the infantile wish (ultimately based upon a command by an Other as well) to have a baby.

Almost anyone is capable of developing a conversion symptom—even psychotics, for whom this symptom, however, does not play a central structuring function. A schizophrenic patient produced "hysterical" pregnancies from time to time, following delusional and hallucinatory experiences in which the Virgin Mary herself commanded her to repopulate the world—even if she was actually unable to become pregnant, as she was not physiologically fertile.

We diagnose a patient as a hysteric of the conversion type if the conversion symptom is the dominant symptom, that is, if the conversion symptom, a "condenser" of jouissance and "what is most real in the subject"

(Lacan's definitions), is what holds the patient together, providing neurotic stability and an unconscious form of personal identity—this, through the retention of a quota of jouissance that the subject condemns but from which she derives a satisfaction (Freud had already coined the formula: the symptom is the sexual life of the neurotic). This is only possible at great cost: a Pyrrhic victory by means of which the unconscious desire finds an alienated way of making itself present. This presentation of the unconscious does not appear to represent desire at all but, on the contrary, suffering and dysfunction; analysis reveals it nevertheless to be desire—desire promoting the strange, extravagant use of the body, which becomes the vehicle of an unconscious drama that makes use of equivocations established in linguistic usage.

This organising yet simultaneously crippling function of the symptom marks the difference between neurosis and psychosis. The neurotic symptom is an alienating attempt at insisting on a form of satisfaction that the subject simultaneously pursues and rejects. The psychotic symptoms of delusions and hallucinations are the desperate attempts at reconstructing a world and a body that are threatened with extinction, where the subject occupies the position of a plaything at the mercy of a tyrannical, persecutory Other.

Anxiety hysteria

The case of little Hans, which has been so instructive as the inaugural case of psychoanalysis with children, inspired Freud to propose a new clinical nosological category within the structure of hysteria: anxiety hysteria.

> In the classificatory system of the neuroses no definite position has hitherto been assigned to "phobias". It seems certain that they should only be regarded as syndromes which may form part of various neuroses and that we need not rank them as an independent pathological process. For phobias of the kind to which little Hans's belongs, and which are in fact the most common, the name of "anxiety-hysteria" seems to me not inappropriate [...]. It finds its justification in the similarity between the psychological structure of these phobias and that of hysteria—a similarity which is complete except upon a single point. That point, however, is a decisive one and well adapted for purposes of differentiation. For

> in anxiety-hysteria the libido which has been liberated from the pathogenic material by repression is not *converted* (that is, diverted from the mental sphere into a somatic innervation), but is set free in the shape of anxiety. In the clinical cases that we meet with, this "anxiety-hysteria" may be combined with "conversion-hysteria" in any proportion. [...] Anxiety-hysterias are the most common of all psychoneurotic disorders. But, above all, they are those which make their appearance earliest in life; they are *par excellence* the neuroses of childhood. (Freud, 1909b, pp. 115–116)

Freud could establish a new diagnostic category because, by the time of the analysis of little Hans, he was well-established in the psychoanalytic discourse that he had introduced some fifteen years earlier. It was the analytic method that enabled him to find a plausible explanation for the states of anxiety and the phobia of the young patient. His conceptual account of the causes of anxiety changed over the years (cf. Freud, 1926d), also on the basis of what he heard from his patients within the framework of the psychoanalytic experience, which required his patient listening, his sensitivity to the equivocations of speech, and his supreme effort at suspending his prejudices and previous knowledge.

Anxiety is an experience during which a state of bodily turmoil suddenly intrudes into the subject's existence, literally upsetting and dislocating her. That this is also a psychological experience simply demonstrates the fact that psychical life takes place in the body, and that through ideas and perceptions it can trigger the state of affective disturbance that is characteristically located in the chest—a feeling of oppression and constriction of the airways, breathlessness and palpitations. Both anxiety and anguish refer etymologically to the notion of "choking". Some colleagues have proposed to employ "anguish" instead of "anxiety", as being closer to the German *Angst* used by Freud and conveying the idea of subjective turmoil and distress more eloquently, whereas the term "anxiety" has been watered down by modern usage and is being applied too loosely to a whole range of human affective states, from very disturbing states of panic to milder experiences of mental malaise.[1] Our colleagues may have a point; but anxiety, anxiety hysteria, anxiety neurosis and related expressions used by psychoanalysts have been around long enough and have become terms well-grounded in clinical and theoretical written works and verbal discussions in the English language.

Jacques Lacan dedicated a year of his Seminar (1962–1963) to anxiety (Lacan, 2013), "the affect of the real", and "the only affect that does not deceive". Affect of the real: because it signals the presence of the real and the lack of resources of the subject facing it—hence the correlative formula of anxiety as "the lack of lack", that is, the lack of the signifier of lack. It is the response to the threat of castration in the most radical acceptation of the term "castration": the threat of total dispossession of the symbolic and imaginary means by which the subject usually deals with the demands that the real imposes—the demands of the drives and those of the external real that impinge upon the living being. For the subject who is confronted by lack but still has the resources to signify it—that is to say, to inscribe it within the chain of signifiers, an operation that makes possible doing something about it—may avoid the experience of anxiety. It is the lack of signifying resources that induces the state of anxiety, well-illustrated by Lacan by his tale of the man confronted by a gigantic female praying mantis, the man not knowing how he himself looks, as he is dressed up in costumes that he is not able to see: it might well be that he looks like a male praying mantis, in which case his fate is not promising, given the peculiar sexual inclinations of the female praying mantis. This fiction is the prototype of situations that generate anxiety in humans: the subject does not know, and is impotent to know, the place that he occupies in the Other's mind; and his own desire, propelled by the activity of his drives, takes him to a position of uncanny contrast between uncertainty (his place in the Other's desire) and the certainty of his death, were he dressed up in the fatal costume.

Lacan retained Freud's nosological categories, which he preferred to call "clinical structures" (Lacan, 1994), even if he made substantial and original contributions to our understanding of those categories. In fact, he introduced only one new category into psychiatric nosology, before becoming a psychoanalyst: self-punitive paranoia. This appeared in his doctoral thesis on paranoic psychosis, and although his rationale for his conceptual proposal already reflects an interest in psychoanalytic theory, it remained in the psychiatric context that inspired it (Lacan, 1975, part II).

As to the category of anxiety hysteria as such, Lacan had little to say; yet his study of anxiety (Lacan, 2013) is a significant contribution to the comprehension of this form of hysteria, and his detailed analyses of the cases of little Hans and Sandy constitutes a substantial revision and original interpretation of the structure and function of phobias (Lacan, 1994; Rodríguez, 1999).

Freud had interpreted phobias (such as the phobia of horses of little Hans) as a kind of spontaneous treatment of anxiety, when this affective state becomes overwhelming and has crippling effects on the subject. He postulated that the first development of what would become a phobic neurosis is a state of generalised anxiety; this is followed by the constitution of a phobic object or situation, usually chosen on the basis of the subject's experience among those objects of his world that are capable of inspiring fear; and finally, the institution of protective measures of avoidance and inhibitions that serve as a barrier against the phobic object. The subject thus finds his existence severely limited by these protective measures, but the state of anxiety is now confined in time and space (see, among other works, the fourth chapter of his metapsychological essay on the unconscious; Freud, 1915e). Usually we call "phobia" the second and third stages of the process, which represent the spontaneous treatment of the initial state of anxiety.

If we take into account that there are means other than a phobia for the treatment of anxiety by the subject herself—without professional assistance—then we may well come to the conclusion that the structure and model of anxiety hysteria is probably the most extended form of neurosis of our times. Non-professional modalities of treatment of anxiety hysteria (as well as a few medical and psychotherapeutic methods) have always been known, but the new forms of human activity, occupation, and entertainment offered by technological advances have greatly expanded the repertoire of "lay" approaches of dealing with anxiety. These approaches are more or less successful in masking anxiety, although the treatment of anxiety might not have been what inspired their development. I am referring to alcohol and drugs (both illegal and medically prescribed), to the social situations in which those substances are consumed (parties and other forms of gathering), as well as other addictive occupations facilitated by the so-called "social media" and the multiple forms of entertainment, information gathering, and masturbatory sexual stimulation available through the Internet. The Internet facilitates modalities of satisfaction that alleviate—yet also generate—anxiety and, in different forms, those modalities of satisfaction have always been known. But the technological novelties introduced by the Internet have multiplied opportunities for anxiolytic, addictive, and, as a rule, solitary activities that distract contemporary neurotics from the common sources of human anxiety—namely, love relations and the demands of work, and in particular the human relations in work places (cf. Rodríguez, 2007). Many commentators on contemporary social life have addressed these new modalities of human troubles; but we are especially interested in their manifestations in the analytic consulting-room. In my own practice, and judging from the accounts of many colleagues in our discussions of real case histories, it is clear that a great number of patients are affected by anxiety hysteria, and suffer from social inhibitions, incipient or ill-defined phobias, and episodes of anxiety with detrimental physiological concomitants that the spontaneous, non-professional forms of treatment (and even conventional medical or psychological treatments) fail to alleviate, or alleviate only partially. If the anxiety is ill-contained, the body suffers: many psychosomatic phenomena arise as a direct consequence of states of anxiety—in particular, cardiovascular illnesses, immunological responses, and other serious pathological developments.

Hysteria and psychosomatic phenomena

The medical category of "psychosomatic disorders" comprises a large number of pathological conditions, with aetiologies that remain obscure in many cases. The respect for the singularity of the patient is a requisite for both the medical practitioner and the psychoanalyst, and is particularly necessary in those cases, as there appear to be no general formulas to elucidate their aetiology and evolution (cf. Leader & Corfield, 2007).

Psychosomatic phenomena should be distinguished from the symptoms of conversion hysteria "proper". In the case of conversion symptoms, the work of psychoanalysis may identify an unconscious causality in a positive way—this, with due consideration of the organic contribution provided by what Freud called "somatic compliance", that is, the preference, on the part of the unconscious, to use those organs and functions of the body that have a history of organic illness as a medium for the expression of a subjective conflict (Freud, 1905e, pp. 40–41). We prefer the use of the expression "psychosomatic phenomena", rather than "psychosomatic symptoms", as the latter term has acquired a specific meaning in psychoanalysis, designating the typical pathological symptomatic manifestations of the neuroses; these involve formations of the unconscious (Lacan's term, which represents a revision of Freud's expression, "compromise formations") plus an unconscious investment in a prohibited yet compulsively pursued form of jouissance (it is in this sense that Freud had spoken of the symptom as "the sexual life of the neurotic"). In using the expression psychosomatic phenomena, we follow the nomenclature preferred by colleagues who have published their specialised research in this area (Guir, 1983; Valas, 1986).

There are, however, points of contact between psychosomatic phenomena, anxiety hysteria, and conversion hysteria. This is due to the fact that the human body, as representation of the living organism, is always open to the influence and manipulations of the unconscious, which in various degrees ultimately also affect the organism. Conversion symptoms exploit the body's plastic capacity to lend its different functions to the dramatic representation of unconscious conflicts. This dramatic representation is metaphoric in its structure: it operates by means of the substitution of a bodily signifier (a bodily organ or function utilised as a signifier) for the signifiers of a conflict under repression, a substitution that engenders a "surplus" of meaning. So, the paralysed leg of a conversion symptom comes to signify, *"Do not take that step"*, thus endowing the affected leg with "extra" meaning or a "surplus" of signification that, normally, the leg does not represent. A metaphoric substitution of this kind is not present in the psychosomatic phenomenon, as this phenomenon is the manifestation of the subject's suffering without the specified meaning of a dramatic unconscious conflict. Yet the *psych* component of the phenomenon refers to the workings of unconscious desire (Lacan, 1977, p. 228). Lacan proposed that the linguistic concept of *holophrase* be applied to psychosomatic phenomena (as well as the subjective positions of the psychotic and the intellectually disabled subject), in so far as these phenomena appear to correspond to a direct, sealed link between unconscious conflicts and the affected organs, without the intermediation of the signifying chain that makes metaphoric substitutions possible (Lacan, 1977, p. 237). The holophrastic arrangement becomes combined with what Lacan characterised as an effect of Pavlov's experiment, based on the fact that a response of the organism may be broken down through a dissection of the circuit involved: the dog's secretion is diverted from the sight of meat to the sound associated with it; the sight of meat is "by-passed" (Lacan, 1977, p. 228). Similarly, the human digestive track may be diverted to respond to a dramatic stimulus, by-passing (foreclosing, one might say) the "natural" phase of the process constituted by the ingestion of food.

Now, the human body's openness to hysterisation, namely, the capacity of this body to represent human dramas in conversions symptoms and normal affective manifestations (Freud, 1909a; 1916–17, Lecture XXV), results in established psychosomatic phenomena being the locus for the superimposition of hysterical symptoms of the conversion type—so that a complex combination of the psychosomatic and the hysteric may well coexist (Rodríguez, 2009; see also in this connection Assoun, 2009 and Soler, 2003).

A patient who suffered from chronic gastric ulcers could, in the course of his analysis, identify the ways in which he aggravated his condition by eating erratically, and especially eating foods that did not agree with his stomach. The analytic interpretations were not specifically aimed at his organic dysfunctions, but at the unconscious constellations that kept him at the mercy of states of anxiety that had been diverted and localised in his digestive system, which thus became the morbid centre of a masochistic jouissance. He could then approach his ulcers in a rational way and, for the first time since the onset of his illness, he was able to follow a proper medical treatment methodically. Yet from time to time his stomach was the arena in which a hysterical process of conversion would develop; he had become "the man with the fragile stomach", and was known as such by relatives and friends. This occurred when his basic neurotic subjective position was mobilised by life circumstances, and the disturbing manifestations in his stomach never reached the severity of his pre-analytic days: they were rather a signal that, as a subject—a subject of the unconscious—he was in trouble.

As "the affect of the real", anxiety is a signal—not a signifier inserted in a chain of signifiers—and this is why it does not deceive. As the signifier is not tied up with any particular meaning, it equivocally refers to a plurality of possible significations. Lacan remarks, however, that anxiety may be absent (Lacan, 1977, p. 41)—which means that it cannot be regarded as an infallible clinical sign. When it is present, it is an unequivocal sign of castration. Yet, from an analytic point of view, this is not the end of our work of elucidation of the unconscious and its formations, but rather the beginning of a possible redirection of the subject's dealings with his/her lack-in-being: towards desire and desiring, as the best available alternative to anxiety.

Anxiety occurs in the living organism and its human symbolic-imaginary representation, the body; in the same body, hysterical conversions emerge, ultimately affecting the organism as well. Can anxiety itself, as psychosomatic phenomena, be hystericised, in the sense of being affected by a process of conversion? Yes, it can. Psychosomatic phenomena, as we have discussed, appear to correspond in many cases to effects of anxiety itself. But "pure" states of anxiety, without concomitant illness in the form of psychosomatic phenomena, are open to becoming affected by the signifiers that the running of human life normally present to the subject. We have already seen that anxiety may be treated through phobias, addictions, and other deflections. A phobia, after all, consists in the transposition of a traumatic encounter with castration on to a newly created dramatic scenario, in which the anxiety is confined to being a "fear of ..." (an object capable of inspiring fear). No amount of spontaneous or psychoanalytic treatment, however, can eliminate the human capacity to develop anxiety, which signals the inevitable confrontation with castration as real and the intrinsic limitations of knowledge, power, and means of satisfaction.

The conversion symptom is located in the body *qua* representation of the living organism and in its extension and intensity is relatively precise, as it is a condition for the equivocality of the unconscious signifiers that sustain it that those signifiers maintain the material identity that defines them *qua* letters; whereas anxiety is the affective response of the living organism to a lack of signifiers when the subject faces a threatening situation—when she "loses the plot", and experiences real castration. The affective response of anguish (or anxiety) operates as a signal for the ego, which is primordially a representation of the body, and thus promotes the defensive functions that attempt to restore the homeostasis of the organism. The neuroses are pathologies in which a state of relative homeostasis is not achieved, or is achieved only partially at the price of chronic symptoms that induce the state of malaise which is their distinctive mark (cf. Freud's *Inhibitions, Symptoms and Anxiety*; 1926d). Anxiety, a response of the organism, ends up affecting the body, and if in the neuroses it becomes chronic, a vicious circle is created, and the symptoms and inhibitions erected to protect the subject from anxiety become a secondary source of anxiety that may well turn out to be more troublesome than the original one.

Depression, so topical in our times and the target of a pharmacological industry that insists on its dangers and continuous expansion, and which is non-specific as a symptom, normally accompanies all forms of neurosis. It has features that combine conversion and anxiety: the body as a whole retreats into a state of affective flatness reminiscent of impotence, while the subject is lost for words and ideas and gives up all hope concerning an Other whose desire is not even enigmatic anymore, as this Other appears to have forsaken her.

At any rate, the body is, in both forms of hysteria, the battle-field of subjective conflicts, and all the outside-the-consulting-room spontaneous attempts at curing them, as well as some forms of treatment inside consulting-rooms, aim at functions of the body—by restricting its movements, avoiding certain encounters, or artificially providing biochemically-induced states of well-being.

Hysteria and perversion

In a remarkable study that preceded Freud's own essay on fetishism, which has remained a paradigm for the psychoanalytic understanding of the perversions (Freud, 1927e), Hanns Sachs compared the structure of phobias and fetishism, illustrating their affinities and differences with clear clinical examples (Sachs, 1986 [1923]). Freud had previously reported at the Vienna Psychoanalytic Society on a case of foot fetishism where the passage from castration anxiety centred on the foot and its transformation into a fetish. This had already alerted psychoanalysts to the links between anxiety hysteria and fetishism, links that are not simply the result of phenomenological comparisons but, more importantly, form the connections between two different subjective positions regarding castration: hysterical and perverse approaches to the same problematic question, experienced in succession (Nunberg & Federn, 1975, pp. 243–246). Sachs' analysis throws light on the possible genesis of perversions, as variations on similar unconscious constellations to those found in hysteria, and the apparent plasticity, at least for some subjects, in the movement from one clinical structure to the other:

> A perversion [...] must have unconscious determinants. Perversion does not exempt anyone from infantile amnesia, which we view as a scar left by large-scale warding off of infantile sexuality. And, in fact, the analysis of a perversion leads as inevitably to unconscious material as does the analysis of a neurosis. In the case of neurosis a repressed fantasy finds expression at the expense of the repressing agency, but only in the form of an ego-dystonic, neurotic symptom; in the case of perversion, a repressed fantasy is capable of becoming

conscious and remaining ego-syntonic and pleasurable. [...] Apart from the change in the pleasure-unpleasure polarity, perversion and neurosis have much in common. Both are outgrowths of infantile sexual life which has been largely overcome and repressed. Both are relatively insignificant residual phenomena of an extensive develop-mental process, conscious representations of unconscious drive vicissitudes. Both merely represent in enlarged and intensified form processes which occur in normal psychic life. A neurotic symptom must be tolerated in consciousness because it affords an adjustment in the disequilibrium between the ego and the repressed. Could it be that the situation is similar for a perversion? [...] Genuine similarity seems most likely to be evident in those cases of perverse satisfaction where the individual accepts only with reluctance and in continuous conflict with moral, religious, and aesthetic compunctions. For these patients, satisfaction itself is, of course, pleasurable, even if limited by abrasive defensive struggles beforehand, and by remorse, shame, and self-condemnation afterwards. We can see an even closer correspondence to the neurotic symptom in those instances in which the certain condition is exceeded. For example, when the satisfaction takes place in reality rather than in fantasy, or when the victim of a sadistic act feels physical pain (while the pleasure is contingent upon sparing such pain), the reaction is by no means neutral. It is not unlike the mechanism of a neurotic symptom: defense with strong components of anxiety occurs [...]. In one case, I was able to follow in detail the transition from a neurotic phobia to a perverse satisfaction. A severely neurotic young woman suffered from a memory that once, when she was half grown, she had beaten a child with sadistic pleasure in the course of playing and in a way that produced no harm. She also remembered that, shortly after puberty, she sometimes at night beat herself on the buttocks and obtained pleasurable sensations in that way. This patient was barely able to utter expressions meaning "beat", especially common nursery words. Every noise reminiscent of beating, such as carpet beating, would drive her wild with repugnance and loathing. After a particularly difficult piece of analysis, masturbation, which had until then been completely repressed, suddenly erupted. The kind of masturbation she engaged in from then on may be considered a form of perverse satisfaction because it took place accompanied exclusively by the fantasy that she was being beaten [...]. Initially, repression of the perverse impulse had produced the phobia; now the phobia was again replaced by the perversion. During the rather lengthy, drawn-out repressive process, which had not begun until after puberty, as well as during that portion of the analytic work during which the repression was being lifted, there were intermediate stages where one could not be sure whether one was dealing with a neurotic symptom or a form of perverse gratification. Such a blending is, in fact, not so very rare an occurrence; for example, a masochistic patient who in general did not limit himself to fantasies, but rather arranged for live events, was nevertheless unable to utter certain slang and nursery expressions which designated his favorite instrument of torture without experiencing vivid feelings of dread. (Sachs, 1986 [1923], pp. 478–480)

The clinical and metapsychological picture described by Sachs is particularly apt to represent the subjective positions of many patients arriving at our doors these days, for whom an initial diagnosis of anxiety hysteria or perversion seems unclear. The distinction between neurosis and perversion is not proportional to that which exists between neurosis and psychosis. The coexistence or successive emergence of neurotic (of the anxiety hysteria type) and perverse clinical organisations is probably more frequent than our pursuit of clearer diagnostic formulations may desire. However, it is also true that there are many patients who consult because of symptoms that belong exclusively to the structure of anxiety hysteria, without any significant development of perverse symptomatology. The presence of neurotic formations that are typical of anxiety hysteria in perverse subjects seems comparatively to be more likely (cf. also Tostain, 1980).

The cultural value of hysteria

Lacan said once that psychoanalysis still remains one of the few discourses that, as a social bond, is available to us (Lacan, 1990, p. 14). A discourse, in the Lacanian sense, constitutes a social bond in which subjects do something to each other, and sometimes what they do is not good for the other or for themselves—but at least they treat each other as subjects, not as machines of production and consumption. In his seminars on the four discourses, Lacan proposed that the discourse of the hysteric is one of the fundamental forms of human discourse identified by psychoanalysis (Lacan, 2007). He thus placed the hysteric's discourse at a level beyond the restricted field of study of the neuroses, and regarded it as the model of the analysand's discourse in the analytic experience and, in a different context, as having a structure analogous to that of science—this, on account of its aiming at the production of knowledge:

$$S \rightarrow S_1$$
$$a \mathbin{/\mkern-2mu/} S_2$$

This "matheme" of the hysteric's discourse is an application of the general formula for discourse:

agent → other

truth // production

This recognition of the value of the hysteric's discourse as a social bond is perhaps based on the share, mentioned earlier, that hysterics had in the creation of psychoanalysis as a method for the investigation of the unconscious. It is not so much a question of praising hysteria—which is after all a neurosis—and hysterics for being neurotic, which requires no particular talents. But it is rather a matter of recognising that which, in the social bond, the hysteric *qua* analysand creates and which testifies to the malaise of our culture, forcing subjectivity to find refuge in conversion symptoms, phobias, and anxiety as desperate means of expressing a human truth that resists repression or suppression. This is a truth that has struggled to be acknowledged since time immemorial, but which, in our times, is denounced by neurotics in their anguish and symptoms. I would add: and this, despite themselves, because a neurotic's search for truth is always biased—biased towards retaining a quota of jouissance that neurotics are reluctant to surrender.

The truth of castration as the defining feature of human sexuality and of the impossibility of a harmonious co-relation between the sexes (Lacan, 1998, p. 59; 2001, p. 365) is a truth somehow inscribed in a hysteric's unconscious. The hysteric remains intolerant of its effects, and exhibits a reluctance to acknowledge it; but in his/her anxiety and symptoms that truth returns, albeit in a disfigured, mutilated form. Freud had already perceived the problematic relation that humans maintain with sexuality, which he variously characterised as a fundamental biological bisexual disposition and as being intrinsically unsatisfying. It was left to Lacan to approach human sexuality as the product of the convergence and disparity of the body, language, and the unconscious, of which hysterics, creatures of such encounters and missed encounters, are the privileged witnesses whose testimonies have enriched psychoanalysis and our culture at large. Even if reluctant to admit it, and even hating it, hysterics have preserved the value of human desire against the seduction of accessible forms of jouissance and the illusion of happiness that they induce.

Note

1. For example, Colette Sepel in her intervention at the English-speaking seminar held in Paris, 28–30 June 2007. The papers presented at that seminar have been published in Anxiety: *The Affect of the Real*, Formations Cliniques du Champ lacanien, Paris, 2009.

References

Adair, M. J. (1997). Plato's lost theory of hysteria. *Psychoanalytic Quarterly*, 66: 98–106.
Assoun, P. -L. (2009). *Corps et Symptôme*. Paris: Anthropos.
American Psychiatric Association (2013). *Diagnostic and Statistical Manual of Mental Disorders, Fifth Edition (DSM-5)*. Washington, DC: American Psychiatric Publishing.
Formations Cliniques du Champ lacanien (2009). *Anxiety: The Affect of the Real*. Paris.
Freud, S. (1893c). Some points for a comparative study of organic and hysterical motor paralyses. *S. E.*, 1: 157. London: Hogarth.
Freud, S. (1984a). The neuro-psychoses of defence. *S. E.*, 3: 41. London: Hogarth.
Freud, S. (1895d) [with J. Breuer]. *Studies on Hysteria. S. E.*, 2. London: Hogarth.
Freud, S. (1900a). The interpretation of dreams. *S. E.*, 4 & 5. London: Hogarth.
Freud, S. (1905e). Fragment of an analysis of a case of hysteria. *S. E.*, 7: 3. London: Hogarth.
Freud, S. (1909a). Some general remarks on hysterical attacks. *S. E.*, 9: 229. London: Hogarth.

Freud, S. (1909b). Analysis of a phobia in a five-year-old boy. *S. E., 10*: 3. London: Hogarth.
Freud, S. (1912b). The dynamics of transference. *S. E., 12*: 99. London: Hogarth.
Freud, S. (1912e). Recommendations to physicians practising psycho-analysis. *S. E., 12*: 111. London: Hogarth.
Freud, S. (1913c). On beginning the treatment (further recommendations on the technique of psycho-analysis, I). *S. E., 12*: 123. London: Hogarth.
Freud, S. (1914g). Remembering, repeating and working-through (further recommendations on the technique of psycho-analysis, II). *S. E., 12*: 147. London: Hogarth.
Freud, S. (1915a). Observations on transference-love (further recommendations on the technique of psycho-analysis, III). *S. E., 12*: 159. London: Hogarth.
Freud, S. (1915e). The unconscious. *S. E., 14*: 159. London: Hogarth.
Freud, S. (1916–17). *Introductory Lectures on Psycho-Analysis. S. E., 15 & 16*. London: Hogarth.
Freud, S. (1917a). A difficulty in the path of psycho-analysis. *S. E., 17*: 137. London: Hogarth.
Freud, S. (1926d). *Inhibitions, Symptoms and Anxiety. S. E., 20*: 77. London: Hogarth.
Freud, S. (1927e). Fetishism. *S. E., 21*. London: Hogarth.
Freud, S. (1930a). *Civilization and its Discontents. S. E., 21*: 59. London: Hogarth.
Guir, J. (1983). *Psychosomatique et cancer*. Paris: Point Hors Ligne.
Lacan, J. (1975). *De la psychose paranoïaque dans ses rapports avec la personnalité*. Paris: Seuil.
Lacan, J. (1977). *The Four Fundamental Concepts of Psycho-Analysis*. London: Tavistock.
Lacan, J. (1990). *Television*. New York: Norton.
Lacan, J. (1994). *Le Séminaire, Livre IV, La relation d'objet, 1956–1957*. Paris: Seuil.
Lacan, J. (1998). *The Seminar, Book XX, Encore, On Feminine Sexuality, the Limits of Love and Knowledge, 1972–1973*. New York: Norton.
Lacan, J. (2001). Allocution sur les psychoses de l'enfant. In: *Autres écrits*. Paris: Seuil.
Lacan, J. (2007). *The Seminar, Book XVII, The Other Side of Psychoanalysis, 1969–1970*. New York: Norton.
Lacan, J. (2013). *The Seminar, Book X, Anxiety, 1962–1963*. London: Polity Press.
Leader, D., & Corfield, D. (2007). *Why Do People Get Ill?* London: Hamish Hamilton.

Nunberg, H., & Federn, E. (Eds.) (1975). *Minutes of the Vienna Psychoanalytic Society, volume IV: 1912–1918*. New York: International Universities Press.

Plato (1961). *The Collected Dialogues of Plato* (Eds. E. Hamilton & H. Cairns). Princeton, NJ: Princeton University Press.

Rodríguez, L. (1999). *Psychoanalysis with Children*. London: Free Association.

Rodríguez, L. (2007). Sexual malaise in the twenty-first century. *Analysis, 13*: 91–97.

Rodríguez, L. (2009). Body parts. *Analysis, 15*: 63–74.

Sachs, H. (1986 [1923]). On the genesis of perversions. *Psychoanalytic Quarterly, 55*: 477–488.

Soler, C. (2003). *L'en-corps du sujet. Transcript of the Course of 2001–2002 at the Collège Clinique de Paris*. Paris: Formations Cliniques du Champ lacanien.

Tostain, R. (1980). Fetishisation of a phobic object. In: S. Schneidermann (Ed.), *Returning to Freud: Clinical Psychoanalysis in the School of Lacan*. New Haven, CT: Yale University Press.

Valas, P. (1986). Horizons de la psychosomatique. In: GREPS (Ed.), *Le phénomène psychosomatique et la psychoanalyse* (Analytica No. 48). Paris: Navarin.

CHAPTER TWO

Hysteria today

Darian Leader

In 1936, a survey at the Vienna Psychoanalytic Clinic showed that out of 3840 cases seen over the previous ten years, there was not a single example of the "grand attack" described by Charcot and witnessed by Freud in the 1880s and 90s (Pisk, 1936). Later commentators would also note the absence of the spectacular symptomology of the Salpêtrière, with the explanation that either hysteria no longer existed or, more commonly, that it had simply changed its form.

The claim that hysteria ceased to exist can hardly be taken seriously for a simple reason. For both Charcot and Freud, the symptoms of hysteria were fabulously changeable. An anaesthesia could transform into a contracture, a paralysis into a neuralgia. What mattered was less the content of the symptom than what place it occupied for the sufferer and what it gave voice to. As anthropologists would soon demonstrate, culture contained "symptom pools" which could be borrowed from in order to articulate a discontent. Deprived of any other means to communicate their malaise or their pain, the subject would use the symptoms available in a culture as "idioms of distress".

"Hysteria today" thus becomes an oxymoron, as the diagnostic category already contains within it a temporal parameter: the symptoms that are historically specific to a given culture at a given time. According to this view, hysteria by definition is constantly updating its symptom pictures. Presenting symptoms will change with culture, but the relation to the symptom will remain invariable, or rather, as invariable as the different categories of hysteria will allow. A robust diagnosis will be predicated not on surface symptomology but on how the subject speaks about their symptom, the position it occupies, and what we can learn about its construction.

* * *

Let's consider three areas here where diagnostic confusion is most acute. We can call them schematically Other Minds, the Other Woman, and the Other Body. They all show us how surface symptoms or motifs in speech can generate too swiftly a diagnosis of hysteria at exactly the points where a differential consideration of hysteria/psychosis should be entertained. By focusing on these points, prejudices can be both clarified and questioned.

To start with the question of Other Minds, a vignette reported by Mustafa Safouan is exemplary. As a young analyst, he was troubled by a patient whose extreme negativity led him to suspect psychosis. On the eve of a holiday period, she made some particularly significant remarks, and then added "I know that you won't say anything since the holidays start tomorrow, and you'll be afraid that what you say might have effects that will go beyond your control" (Safouan, 2000).

Telling this to his friend, Lucien Israel, the latter replied that anyone who could recognise their dependence on the speech of the other could never be psychotic. We might think, on the contrary, that such an awareness is in equal measure indicative of psychosis. While avoiding giving any diagnostic value to the analysand's comment in the absence of further details of the case, we could note how an understanding of the effects of speech is precisely one of the most basic features of psychosis. Calculating, pondering, or intuiting what is on the Other's mind is not solely a sign of hysterical identification with a lack in the Other, but can also be the vehicle of a necessary manoeuvre for a psychotic subject, to be able to better situate him or herself and create a boundary to the Other. In some cases, it can also be a consequence of the absence of such boundaries.

The prejudice here is to accord to hysteria a unique alertness to the question of Other Minds, always trying to figure out what value the subject has for the Other. This is a fundamental misconception of hysteria. A perpetual questioning of one's value can characterise any number of cases of psychosis, the difference with hysteria being the place this enquiry occupies: whether it is predicated on the castration complex or on an openness to the Other.

We must remember here that one of the defining features of the group of schizophrenias is that questions of meaning tend to be left open. A psychotic subject may spend their whole life in the unbearable situation of not knowing what they are for the Other, perhaps made worse by the certainty that this Other is watching them, maligning them, or judging them at all times. A manifest concern with the desire of the Other tells us very little, until we have gone on to explore exactly what function it has. Freud has indeed evoked in a discussion at the Vienna Psychoanalytic Society "those cases that are initially hysterias and later turn into dementia [praecox]s, as soon as the hysteric mechanism of defence is no longer able to do its job" (Nunberg & Federn, 1975, p. 278).

Many psychotic subjects use the desire of the Other to stabilise, using the hysterical "*dérobade*" to maintain a tolerable position. What seems on the surface to be a behaviour of slipping away, of stoking the desire of the Other, of creating any number of unsatisfied desires in the world around them, turns out to be a way of creating the distance necessary for the subject to survive. The Other must be kept at an artificial distance, which the subject has constructed. Playing the hysteric here can introduce the equilibrium that a psychotic subject requires.

Saying "No" to the Other, eluding the Other's efforts at mastery and containment, or, more generally, refusing to place oneself in the position of object for the Other can be, very simply, precisely that: an attempt to avoid objecthood. Where, for the hysteric, such refusals serve to perpetuate the question of their value for the Other, in psychosis this is a secondary effect. The subject's actions do not aim primarily at creating a question but at limiting the Other's proximity.

This kind of slipping away is in fact quite different from that classically associated with hysteria. The limits to contact and intimacy may be a way of avoiding the risk of psychical and bodily dissolution. In hysteria, on the contrary, the subject may aim at the Other's love while refusing the sexual consequences of this love. Hence the range of symptoms we see here, ranging from difficulties of genital and bodily arousal to impasses of reproduction and hormonal, bacterial, and viral symptomology.

* * *

The relation to the Other here aims at a point of desire, of lack, which the subject identifies with, beyond any imaginary identifications that may be at play. And this brings us to the second point of diagnostic confusion. The hysteric's identification with the lack they have unveiled is generally situated in the father, and this tends to be in inverse proportion to the magnification of a female Other. The presence of an Other woman may be clinically obvious, while the paternal identification is more discreet, despite Freud's well-known error in the Dora case.

We could schematise this in the following way:

Symptom → Father as empowered (P+) → Father as lacking (P-) → Lack in mother (M-)

We might also consider the consequences for the subject of the point at which the magnification occurs. Situated between (P+) and (P-) or between (P-) and (M-) is not the same thing.

It is puzzling that commentaries on the Dora case rehearse endlessly the standard Lacanian arguments, without looking for anything else in the material. Freud's undervaluation of Mrs K. meant that he missed the place of the Other Woman, defined as the primary site of the hysteric's interest. The unfortunate result of this has been that an often hasty diagnosis of hysteria follows from the central place of an Other Woman in clinical material. If the subject shows excessive curiosity, love, or desire for some female figure, the category follows almost as a given.

Freud had of course pointed out in his paper on "Female sexuality" that the earliest "phase of attachment to the mother is especially intimately related to the aetiology of hysteria, which is not surprising when we reflect that both the phase and the neurosis are characteristically feminine, and further, that in this dependence on the mother we have the germ of later paranoia in women" (Freud, 1931, p. 227). The "intense and passionate" link to the mother here is associated with both hysteria and psychosis.

In psychosis, indeed, the Other Woman will often have a central place, whether in the form of an imaginary other that the subject follows blindly, of a real Other that the subject must keep in their sights in order to remain as safe as possible, of an erotomanic consistency that the subject needs in order to maintain their own position, or simply as any avatar of the mother, magnified precisely due to the absence of any principle of limitation. We could think here of Lacan's Aimée, whose life was filled with female figures who took on a quality for her that was both vertiginous and enigmatic.

It is worth considering here the place of the Other Woman in hysteria itself. Freud might have misjudged the importance of Mrs. K., but what place did the latter really hold? An embodiment of the mystery of femininity, perhaps, but what did Dora's passionate gravitation towards her protect her from? Perpetuating the hysteric's question, yes, but isn't there also an unspeakable horror for the hysterical subject in the Other's enjoying without her? As Lacan observed, the hysteric believes in an absolute jouissance, which means one that excludes her. This can be imagined as a feasting on human flesh or on food, and is one of the reasons why—beyond the manifest competition between desire and demand—eating disturbances are so common here.

* * *

Let's move to our third theme, the Other body. Although we have seen how hysterical symptoms are variable over time, all of the phenomena catalogued in Freud's (1888) piece for Villaret's encyclopedia are still to be found in abundance today. What has changed is just that they are not found in the same places. Convulsive attacks, disturbances of bodily sensibility and sensory activity, paralysis, and contractures are still incredibly common, but they cluster in neurology consultations, GP surgeries, and pain clinics.

Referral to psychotherapists, let alone psychoanalysts, is quite rare here, and the symptoms tend to lead to rounds of consultation with specialists. The body remains Other, the site of an unexplained and pervasive misery. After months or years of inconclusive care, the symptom may either settle into chronicity or metamorphose into something else. By this time, medical interest in the individual's case will have waned, staff will have changed, and the symptom will be lost in the neverending process of local intervention. This process will also block any gathering of real data about the vicissitudes of conversion.

When such phenomena do come to analytic attention, the diagnostic issue is often confused. Freud was quite clear as early as the *Studies on Hysteria* that if the mechanism of conversion is direct, we may be in the field not of neurosis but psychosis. If a word or an image imprints itself on the body without passing through the ciphering mechanisms of repression, we are dealing with less a classical hysterical conversion than a "symbol", to use one of Freud's terms. The clearer the symptomatic construction, the less likely that it is predicated on repression.

Sometimes, complaints about the suffering body may invite the idea of hysteria, but it is always prudent to ask whether the apparent conversion hides a hypochondria or a porosity of bodily boundaries. Does the concern with the body reveal a fixity or shifts in signification? If we take Dora once again as an example, we find a chain of signifiers which moves from the conversion symptom to the father's castration. We could contrast this with the bodily phenomena of psychosis which may follow a different logic. The clinical question here is whether castration is the operator of symptom formation or not.

Privation, for example, may be foregrounded in the clinical picture of both neurosis and psychosis, but the broadcasting of dissatisfaction has no diagnostic significance until the presence or absence of this operator is verified. The rigidity of a complaint may be the vehicle of a paranoiac belief just as its flexibility may be the sign of a schizophrenic drift. If the sense of privation is indeed dialectised by castration, the structure will be different, marked by what Lacan called the "supple chain" of the phantasy (Lacan, 1960).

Likewise, phenomena of both the presence and absence of bodily sensibility must be carefully explored. The sense of disconnection from the body, for example, can be found across diagnostic structures. Let's take two examples. In the first, a young woman who complains of multiple bodily woes describes the sensation of disassociation from her body, as if she were standing next to herself. Contextualising these episodes shows that they are linked to the moments when her father created a distance from her, as if the femaleness of his daughter's body was not bearable for him. A dream follows in which she has been shot, blood pours from her body, and her father insists that she stop the bleeding.

In Herbert Rosenfeld's celebrated case of Mildred, his analysand feels dead, cut off from the world and from herself (Rosenfeld, 1947). There is a fear of falling into an unconscious state, and the sense that there is a blanket separating her from the world. Rosenfeld tends to interpret everything in terms of love and hate directed to his own person. As she describes "swelling up like a balloon" and senses that *"expectancy had something to do with it"*, he takes this to be a representation of the fear of himself being forced into her. The evocation of pregnancy is totally ignored, as is the question of the mother's desire for her child, despite the many other indications in the clinical material. Similarly, the representations of "deadness" often allude to Mildred's beloved brother, killed during the war, yet these are not taken up into the thread of the analysis.

The interest of these examples, however, lies in their indeterminacy. Neither phenomenon of disconnection from the body is in itself categorical diagnostically. Both cases involve the experience of the body, both cases involve some sort of registration of the desire of the Other, and both cases point to questions of sexual identity. Yet the link of a symptom to either of these latter two motifs is compatible with both a diagnosis of hysteria and psychosis. It is less the link as such than the place that this link occupies. In the Mildred case, we are not in the best position to judge this, as essentially what we witness is an analysand desperately defending herself against a barrage of interpretations from an analyst who can only see reflections of himself in his patient. It is worth remembering here that plenty of psychotic subjects are troubled by questions of femininity and masculinity, without arriving at fixed binary solutions.

The hysteric is not the only subject allowed to pose a question about their sexual identity, just as the hysteric is not the only one with a sensitivity to the desire of the Other or a claim to use the body as a space for conversion. It is less the presence of these motifs that truly characterises hysteria than the nature of the space in which they are elaborated. If the medium of this space is lack, and, crucially, if it is lack that operates identification of elements in this space, we are probably with hysteria. It is this space of hysteria, rather than any historical time, that can shed light on the structure of symptoms and the particular mode of subjective division that it involves.

References

Freud, S. (1888). Hysteria. *S. E.*, *1*: 41–59 London: Hogarth.
Freud, S. (1931). Female sexuality. *S. E.*, *21*: 225–243. London: Hogarth.
Lacan, J. (1960). The subversion of the subject and dialectic of desire in the Freudian unconscious. In: B. Fink (Trans.), *Écrits* (pp. 671–702). London: Norton, 2006.
Nunberg, H., & Federn, E. (Eds.) (1975). *Minutes of the Vienna Psychoanalytic Society, Vol 4*. New York: IUP.
Pisk, G. (1936). Über die Änderung der hysterischen Symptome in den letzten Jahren. *Wiener klinische Wochenschrift*, 2:938–939.
Rosenfeld, H. (1947). Analysis of a schizophrenic state with depersonalization. In: *Psychotic States* (pp. 13–33). London: Hogarth, 1965.
Safouan, M. (2000). Pour mémoire, Lucien Israël et l'hystérique. *La Clinique Lacanienne*, 2; 213–214.

CHAPTER THREE

Beyond queer?

Anne Worthington

*What is hysteria? And what does psychoanalysis
have to say about it today?*

A young woman consulted an analyst as she was unable to come to a decision as to whether to join her lover, who had taken up a prestigious job in another country. Some weeks later, she described how she had been referred to an "ear, nose and throat" specialist as she had difficulties in swallowing. Careful questioning by the analyst elicited the information that her symptom originated with the news of the death of her beloved baby brother (as she referred to him) in a road traffic accident. The analyst, familiar with the many psychoanalytic commentators (for example: Appignanesi, 2008; Bollas, 2000; Moncayo, 2008; Verhaeghe, 2004) who have discussed the disappearance of hysteria into new diagnostic categories, was surprised to hear that the ENT specialist diagnosed globus hystericus. Indeed, the disappearance of hysteria is also a contemporary theme for non-psychoanalytic clinicians[1]. Furthermore, the diagnosis of globus hystericus itself, characterised by a feeling of a lump in the throat, and/or difficulties with swallowing, associated with anxiety or "severe life events" (Harris, Deary, & Wilson, 1996) without a detectable underlying organic condition, which is more frequently found in women, is beginning to transmute into different diagnostic terms, for example, globus sensation or, more succinctly, just referred to as globus. And, perhaps unsurprisingly, reduced to just hystericus. Nevertheless, perhaps like hysteria itself, with its plasticity of symptoms that reflect the expectations of its historical and cultural context, up it pops again as a descriptive category, to name the as yet unspoken suffering of this twenty-first century woman in a twenty-first century London hospital.

This modern-day example illustrates something of the persistence of the associations to hysteria from its earliest history with Plato's description of wandering wombs, which associates hysteria with women, unsatisfied sexual desire, and frustrated reproduction. Freud and Breuer, too, responding to the challenge of hysteria, observed the plasticity of their patients' symptoms and, like our modern-day therapist above, understood the seemingly inexplicable symptom as a communication about a trauma—a trauma linked to a frustration of libidinal impulses. The psychoanalytic treatment reported in Studies on Hysteria was concerned with the alleviation of symptoms, but it was also concerned with the reconstruction of their patients' histories, which gave access to a knowledge about desire, a desire so strongly prohibited by the patients' own ideas about what was acceptable, whether socially or according to their ideas about who they were, that it had been repressed only to emerge in bodily symptoms. Dora's case—and that of the homosexual girl—demonstrated the universality of bisexuality that is evident in the conflicts experienced in every subject's assumption of her own sex. Freud's research and treatment of hysteria, as is well documented, led to his formulations of the unconscious, fantasy, identification, repression, the Oedipus complex, castration, transference, resistance—indeed all psychoanalysis's principal discoveries (Laplanche & Pontalis, 1973, p. 195).

But what do psychoanalysts today have to say about hysteria? Well, there appears to be some agreement that hysteria exists, although this claim is often surrounded by commentary about its disappearance as a diagnostic category. Its disappearance is variously explained as a consequence of the inconsistency of its presentation, or of the hostility of feminist critique, and by a modern reluctance or caution with regard to psycho-diagnostics—supported by the argument that to account for the profound differences between people is somehow dehumanising or discriminatory, along with the contemporary predilection for fluidity, for an antipathy to a fixed or static hypothesis. Lacanian psychoanalysis is said, on the other hand, to have maintained a sustained interest in theorising hysteria[2]. Lacanians, who don't all "sing from the same hymn sheet" on every aspect of psychoanalytic theory and practice, do work with a clearly defined system of psycho-diagnostics. For Lacanians—following Freud—there is a distinction between the neuroses and the psychoses and the distinction is made clear by an analysis of how we make sense of the experience of being human, what we do with our bodies and sex, and how we position ourselves in relation to the Other. Thus a diagnosis of hysteria is not dependent on somatic symptoms, nor on other phenomena frequently associated with hysteria, such as theatricality, eroticisation, or suggestibility. The analysis of the speech of the patient, and of the transference (which may display such characteristics), will guide diagnosis.

According to Lacan "the structure of a neurosis is essentially a question'" (1993, p. 174). The question that distinguishes hysteria from the other neuroses is a question about sex: Am I a man or a woman? What is a woman? Or as Patricia Gherovici reports as being the current question in the clinic of hysteria: "Am I straight or am I bisexual? Am I a man or a woman?" (2010, p. xii). Or from my own clinic: "Am I gay, or queer, or homosexual? What kind of man am I?" It is a question that has been raised in a myriad of guises, which have always reflected the zeitgeist. This return of a question—reiterated, repeated to assume a desired form—itself mirrors something of the hysteric's desire, bound up as it is with the desire of the Other.

In brief, the hysteric-to-be (the infant), like other neurotics-to-be, looks to the Other (the mother) to supply the answer its needs. Being totally dependent on this (m)Other, the "hysteric-to-be" needs to understand what it is the Other wants: if "me-to-be" gives her what she wants, she will relieve my bodily needs/libidinal drives. The "hysteric-to-be" identifies with the signifiers of the (m)Other's desire, only to find that she can't provide satisfaction. Total satisfaction is an impossibility. It is the price of moving from being a "to be" to being human, to being a "speaking-being". Nevertheless, she will still try elsewhere. Freud theorised this problem of becoming human, of subjectivity, in terms of the Oedipus complex and castration. The child sacrifices her primary love-object in favour of an identification with the father, the representative of the law. This second Other, as Verhaeghe (2004) helpfully names him, will either disqualify himself or be disqualified from the position of the one that has the answer to the question of the dissatisfactions of being human. The hysteric becomes particularly attuned to investigating what it is that the Other wants, while at the same time setting up another figure who knows what is wanted, and is deemed to have it.

Let's illustrate these puzzling ideas from contemporary published case material. Two major contributions on hysteria by practicing English analysts were published in 2000: Christopher Bollas' *Hysteria* and Juliet Mitchell's *Mad Men and Medusas*. They conceive of hysteria differently. For Mitchell, the hysteric is someone whose narcissism has been ruptured by the first lateral relations, those with our siblings. Bollas argues that sexuality is traumatic for all children as it destroys the relation to the mother, and the hysteric opposes the knowledge that "mother" has transformed into sex object.

Bollas' clinical example, "Heather", provides a helpful illustration of the hysteric's position in relation to the desire of the Other, and how diagnosis is reached through an analysis of the transference. Heather (Bollas, 2000, pp. 158–160), is a "social worker" and diagnosed as "borderline" (ibid., p. 158). It is a central part of Bollas' thesis, in common with much of the commentary on the disappearance of hysteria, that the new and increasingly popular diagnosis of borderline personality disorder is but a new name for hysteria. Heather's analyst, Jerome, had a good reputation but was isolated in so far as there were "few psychoanalysts in his neck of the woods" (ibid.). Heather was a perfect patient for many years. She "flowered", she promoted her analyst's work and referred patients to him (ibid.). Jerome reported to his colleagues that he found Heather to be "clinically significant" (ibid.). Heather declared her love for Jerome and her wish to marry him, which Jerome attempted to interpret as an "expression of a new-found sense of self" while at the same time promising that their relationship would not end with the end of the analysis. Jerome and Heather went on to present academic papers together and "seemed colleague-like" (ibid., p. 159). Jerome understood the gratifying transformation of his patient "from an attractive, somewhat diffident woman to a stunningly dressed person and a passionate advocate of psychoanalysis" (ibid., p. 158) as evidence that "she was being empowered through auxiliary ego work on the part of her analyst" (ibid.). Bollas, the author and we, the readers, are not surprised by the dénouement to this tale (unlike Jerome, sadly—who has not responded to her sexual overtures) Heather reports him to his professional regulators for sexually assaulting her.

This case of hysteria today provides a succinct illustration of the structure of hysteria. Heather is a social worker—like Breuer's Anna O. Social work provides the perfect opportunity for the hysteric to please others, for self-sacrifice in an attempt to relieve the anxiety of dissatisfaction by satisfying the Other. And at the same time, the clients of social workers are those who are abused and exploited by the Other, thus confirming the hysteric's view of the failures of that Other. Heather, during her six years of analysis, determines what it was that the Other, in the person of Jerome, desired, and identifies with that desire, appropriating it as her own. Her symptoms reflect the clinical interests of her analyst and she makes gratifying progress during the treatment. She becomes professionally successful, presenting papers at conferences—presumably learning from her analysis. It is she, appropriating the desire of her analyst, who is the advocate of psychoanalysis and who finds new patients. Furthermore, she successfully—according to the account of Jerome's confession to his peer supervision group—embodies his sexual fantasies with her "sexually revealing outfits" (ibid., p. 159). She becomes his kind of desirable woman. The false allegation illustrates what Lacan has called *"revendication"*, the other side of self-sacrifice—as Heather reclaims what is hers and Jerome is removed from his pedestal.

Juliet Mitchell, too, explains hysteria as a response to Oedipal conflicts. Her fictionalised case of Mrs. P (Mitchell, 2000, pp. 226–231) describes the ways in which the gender question: "Am I a man or a woman?" becomes evident in the analysis, through the patient's reports of her dreams and in fantasies. Mrs. P suffered from shaking fits—as if she was shivering with cold—and eating disorders, a sensation of choking and many phobias. Mitchell interprets the dreams and fantasies of fragmentation as a protest. The shaking and fragmentation into different personalities are also interpreted as a protest—not a protest, as some feminist commentators might have it, about her social conditions, but a protest, a refusal to be displaced and thus disappeared by another object of the (m)Other's interest. Mrs. P's father had died before she was six years old and she imagined him "as a homunculus, a little man, inside her" (ibid., p. 229). She identified with what she perceived as her stepfather's desire, and became his son and heir. By becoming a boy, she was also able to "outbid her sister". Once a "natural son" (ibid., p. 228) was born, Mrs. P again became a girl to "outbid her brother".

While these two brief illustrations exemplify some contemporary ideas, there is frequently an antipathy detectible in the writings about hysteria. Verhaeghe (2004, pp. 372–373) points out that the hysteric is frequently charged with being "a 'prick tease' … manipulative, a fake, a hypocrite …". Or, as Bollas (2000, p. 173) puts it, hysterics seem "messed up and bonkers". Could the antipathy that reveals itself in the writings of psychoanalysts be a response, not only to the mysterious language of the conversion symptoms, but also to other characteristics of hysteria—the appropriation of the Other's desire? Hysterics, from this perspective, appropriate the Other's desire by identifying with it, but the Other is always found wanting. To return to our young woman with the lump in her throat—she had sacrificed a great deal to support her lover's career, only to conclude that she really hadn't been worth the effort. Bollas describes this identification with the Other as "showing off" (2000, p. 107) illustrating his thesis with the stereotype of the camp gay man who has honed his skills "from countless acts of fulfilling the imagined object of the other's desire, in which the true self is suspended whilst a stand-in takes its place" (ibid., p, 118). The charge that hysterics over-eroticise and are seductive is also explained by a concern with the Other's desire, with the aim of proving that the Other is wanting "it" from them. For Mitchell (2000, pp. 134–135) it is not so much antipathy, but rather that hysteria is "intolerable"; there is something "that repels thought about hysteria". She describes the hysteric as having the "charm of the small child" (ibid.) but "with something deadly there". This idea of the hysteric as having two sides—the moral, rational, conforming side and on the other, the sexual, crazy, and evil—has a long history. Was it not this idea that was demonstrated in Charcot's expositions at the Salpêtrière? For Mitchell, the hysteric's "rampant, seductive sexuality" is explained by the sexualisation of the death drive (ibid.).

Hysteria today, then, is perhaps not quite so different from the hysteria of yesterday: the somatic symptoms are messages, expressions of something repressed, questions addressed to the Other; it is associated with sex and sexuality, feminine sexuality; and the inherent bisexuality of the neurotic manifests itself in the hysteric's speech, dreams, and identifications. Borossa (2001) draws our attention to another dimension of the way in which hysteria is thought about today: the mass phenomena such as screaming girls at pop concerts, football fans, and those braying for the blood of paedophiles. A more discreet example is the outbreak of a mysterious illness amongst teenage girls at high school in

New York in 2011–12, an account of which has since been fictionalised (Abbott, 2014). The novel seems to indicate that there's not much new in the way we think about hysteria today, with its themes of quests for sexual knowledge, sexuality of teenage girls, somatic symptoms, identification, and the sexual intrigues and problems of parents, all resonating with Freud's story of Dora of 1905 (1905e).

What is queer? And what does it have to say about psychoanalysis?

Queer theory and queer activism are commonly ascribed to a dissatisfaction with identity politics and as a response to the political marginalisation and pathologisation of homosexuality. But could not the emergence of queer be read as a twentieth/twenty-first century response to hysteria, in a similar way that psychoanalysis itself is a response to hysteria? If, as Borossa argues (2001, p. 8), "psychoanalysis is the logical outcome of the questions that hysteria had been asking thought the centuries about gender, conflict and power", is not queer the logical outcome of hysteria's questions of the century post-psychoanalysis?

Unlike psychoanalysis, queer theory is not a clinical discourse. Nevertheless, in that it is concerned with desire, repression, gender, subjectivity, identity, representation, knowledge, power, sexuality, and sexual practice, it shares similar scholarly concerns with psychoanalysis. Furthermore, the texts produced by queer theorists, document political and epistemological changes that are underpinned by accounts of human misery, which are also the concern of psychoanalysis.

Commentators on queer theory agree on the difficulties with the definition of queer theory. Indeed, this is a discourse that is "not concerned with definition, fixity or stasis but is transitive, multiple and anti-assimilationist" (Salih, 2002, p. 9). It is a theory that is "conceptually slippery" (Turner, 2000, p. 3) and that "struggles to remain in the process of (un)becoming" (Sullivan, 2003, p. v). It "is an ensemble of knowledges, many of them contesting knowledges. A site of struggle not a monolithic discourse" (Hennessy, 2000, p. 53). It "is a species of post-structuralism and deconstruction" (Sinfield, 2005, p. ix), that "refers not only to the objects of speculation—lesbian, gay and other forms of sexuality intolerable to the heterocentric mainstream—but perhaps more interestingly to the ways in which they are treated and the knowledges that deal with them" (Grosz, 1994, p. 157, n.3). While the term "queer" has a substantial etymology that refers to phenomena and objects regarded as odd or strange, differing from the normal, "suspicious, dubious [...] unbalanced mentally [...]" (Collins English Dictionary, 1994, p. 1271), or as states of giddiness or fainting—arguably, the most immediate association in the English-speaking world of the late twentieth century is to its informal and derogatory use as referring to a "homosexual, usually a male" (ibid.). The appropriation of the derogatory term by homosexual men came about within the context of a "liberationist" politics, echoing the appropriation of racist terms. It is curious that the term "queer" should be deployed ignoring its associations with male homosexuality, as if it were non-gendered, when in fact it is a term that was taken up by those who were dissatisfied with the identities associated with "gay" and "lesbian" politics, both terms referring also to women. De Lauretis (1991) holds that the queer's project was to produce "another discursive horizon—another way of thinking the sexual" (ibid., p. iv). In her introduction to the queer theory issue of differences (1991), she provides a useful account of the genesis and function of the label "queer" and its own self-understanding as defiant, transgressive, post-modern:

> Today we have on the one hand, the terms lesbian and gay to designate distinct kinds of life-styles, sexualities, sexual practices, communities, issues, publications and discourses; on the other hand the phrase "gay and lesbian" or more frequently "lesbian and gay" (ladies first) has become standard currency ... QT was arrived at in the effort to avoid all of these fine distinctions in our discursive protocols, not to adhere to any one of the given terms, not to assume their ideological liabilities, but instead to both transgress and transcend—or at least problematise them. (cited by Grosz, 1994, p. 257, n.3)

Hennessy (2000) argues that queer theory "is particularly well suited to a capitalist regime of hyperconsumption and accumulation that recasts the boundaries between psyche and social, private and public, nation and colony, body and market in order to produce desire as a transnational-sexual-psychic-commodity structure" (ibid., p. 195). In her view, psychoanalysis is central to this project. Her reading of the key texts of queer theory situates psychoanalysis as pivotal in the creation of "founding myths" (ibid., p. 194) of individualism, myths based on notions of the "bourgeois family" (ibid., p. 181). And although she acknowledges the importance of psychoanalysis for the understanding of psychic processes, in her view, it also remains an extremely effective technology for remapping the modern capitalist self—both clinically and theoretically (ibid.). Some psychoanalysts indeed give weight to a model of psychic well-being that reflects the dominant ideology of the time. Yet, a clinical practice that seeks to analyse the individual and to explore specific solutions to the problem of being a desiring human subject frequently finds itself opposed to prevailing norms—Freud's refusal to pathologise or seek to cure homosexuality being a case in point.

Queer theory is informed by Foucauldian theory and methodology; yet, while it is alert to Foucault's critique of psychoanalytic discourse in the production and construction of homosexuality, it is less explicitly engaged with his analysis of hysteria. In *The History of Sexuality*, Michel Foucault (1976) describes the "hysterization of women's bodies" as one of the crucial features of psychiatric and medical power. "Hysterization" was "a three-fold process whereby the feminine body was analyzed ... as being thoroughly saturated with sexuality; whereby it was integrated into the sphere of medical practices, by means of a pathology intrinsic to it; whereby, finally, it was placed in organic communication with the social body [...] the family space [...] and the life of children; the Mother, with her negative image of 'nervous woman' constituted the most visible form of this hysterization" (Foucault, 1976, p. 104). Foucault is far less interested in the characteristics of hysteria than in how she is transformed into an object for knowledge and control.

Queer theory's deployment of Foucault, whilst not dismissing his analysis of psychoanalytic discourse—discourse being defined as that which both constructs and simultaneously controls—in the construction of gender and sexuality, still makes use of psychoanalysis' conceptual tools. The contributions of psychoanalysis cannot be ignored. For example, Butler's argument that sex/gender is discursively constructed is not so far from psychoanalysis—in which sex and gender are the effects of language on the body—but she reads psychoanalysis as a key player in the reinforcement of the "binary, heterosexist framework that carves up genders into masculine and feminine and forecloses an adequate description of the kinds of subversive and parodic convergences that characterize gay and lesbian cultures" (1990, p. 84).

Judith Butler's intervention on the question of "gender"—the "inscription of meaning on a pregiven sex" (1990, p. 11)—is one such response from queer theory. Butler, informed by a Foucauldian perspective, was motivated by her concern that feminists' assumption that all women were as one, marginalising homosexual women—or more precisely those women who were not heterosexual (ibid., p. vii). If gender is socially constructed, so is sex: the "production of sex as the prediscursive ought to be understood as the effect of the apparatus of cultural construction designated by *gender*" (ibid., p. 11). She formulates the question "Am I a man or a woman?" slightly differently as "What gender are you?" and asks whether gender is something you can have (ibid.). For Butler too there is a question of "being" or "having".

Her gendered subject is a performative construction, a subject constructed in discourse by the acts it performs. And, like Foucault's homosexuals, criminals, and the insane, gendered subjects are simultaneously constructed and controlled by discourse and prohibition that must be analysed in the historical, epistemological contexts in which they arise. "Gender proves to be performative—that is, constituting the identity it is purported to be. In this sense, gender is always a doing, though not a doing by a subject who might be said to pre-exist the deed" (ibid., p. 25). Identity is a "doing"; it is not a performance by a subject but a "set of repeated acts within a highly rigid regulatory frame that congeal over time to produce the appearance of substance, of a natural sort of being" (ibid., p. 33). The "repeated acts" are speech acts. Thus, gender identities are constructed by language, and the subject is an effect of language: "That the gendered body is performative suggests that it has no ontological status apart from the various acts which constitute it" (ibid., p. 136). The thesis of *Gender Trouble* implicitly draws on Austin's (1975) speech act theory and Derrida's deconstruction, and is later more explicitly elaborated by Butler in *Bodies That Matter* (1993). In this text, that which is performative is the result of interpellation and citation: "the constative claim is always to some degree performative" (ibid., p. 11).

Butler is interested in the political possibilities that emerge from an understanding of gender as an effect of discourse, practices, and institutions instead of as a fact of nature. She advocates a disruption of the naturalisation of the notion of gender by means of a displaced repetition of its performativity, which would draw attention to those processes that consolidate dual identities. One of the strategies she recommends is a parodic repetition of gender norms. Instead of marking a distance between itself and the parodied original, the kind of parody that she has in mind is a parody "of the very notion of an original" (Butler, 1990, p. 175). In her view, the performance of drag draws attention to the imitative nature of gender itself and it will thus destablise "the naturalized categories of identity and desire" (ibid., p. 177). The domains of gender and sexuality are not organised in terms of originality and imitation. What they manifest, instead, is the endless—though heavily regulated—possibilities of performativity.

Butler's concern is with gender and sexual identities rather than the sexed subjectivity of psychoanalysis. Thus, her account of homosexuality and heterosexuality as elaborated in *Gender Trouble* (1990) is an account of identity, which draws on Foucault's notion that homosexuality is produced by prohibitive discourse as well as on the Freudian theory of the Oedipus complex. Butler argues that gender identity is the result of the internalisation of a prohibition of homosexuality in infancy, a prohibition that precedes the heterosexual incest taboo of the Freudian account. In *Gender Trouble*, she addresses questions that stem from her reading of Freud's "Mourning and melancholia" (1917) and *The Ego and The Id* (1923). In 1923 Freud explains the infant's desire for either the mother or the father as being the result of "dispositions". He writes: "[the girl] will bring her masculinity into prominence and identify with her father ... instead of with her mother. This will clearly depend on whether the masculinity in her disposition—whatever that may consist of—is strong enough" (ibid., p. 32). Butler's question is: "What are these primary dispositions on which Freud himself apparently founders?" (Butler, 1990, p. 77), on which she concludes that these are not innate— as she thinks Freud said—and are the effects, rather than the causes, of identifications. Through her reading of Freud's 1917 and 1923 papers, she argues that the prohibited, and thus lost, parental object is also a "prohibiting or withholding object of love" (Butler, 1990, p. 80). The function of the ego ideal, she claims, is to "inhibit or repress" (ibid.) the desire for the parent. Further, through the mechanism of internalisation, its function is to "preserve that love" (ibid.). Thus "gender identification is a kind of melancholia" (ibid.), through which the prohibiting object is internalised as a prohibition. At this point, Butler introduces the notion of a taboo against homosexuality that is prior to the incest taboo— a "taboo [that] in effect creates the heterosexual "dispositions" by which the Oedipal conflict becomes possible" (ibid., p. 82). For Butler, then, all gender identity is the result of the homosexual taboo; and if heterosexuality is formed on the basis of a primary loss of the same-sexed parent, and melancholia is the response to that loss, heterosexuality and heterosexual identity cannot but be melancholic.

An account of sexed subjectivity is at the cornerstone of psychoanalysis. But, at least as exemplified in Butler's work, queer theory does not have such an account of its own: "One cannot account for subjectivation, and in particular the becoming of one's subjection, without recourse to a psychoanalytic account" (Butler, 1997, p. 87). I cite this example of Butler's account of how and who we choose to love, to suggest that queer takes up hysteria's response to the difficulties of being human, of being a man or a woman, of what to do about sex, and where to position oneself in relation to others and the Other—in the context of its genesis in today's post-psychoanalytic world.

Queer-steria: What are the resonances with queer and hysteria?

The productive engagement of queer theory and psychoanalysis is quite recent. Today there is a current within queer theory that engages with psychoanalysis to posit new theorisations of subjectivity, identity, and desire, and to propose new conceptualisations of homosexuality. Other queer theorists take up psychoanalytic theory to advance and augment a project that challenges the dominant socio-political culture, particularly with regard to sex and sexuality. It was more than forty years ago that the American Psychiatric Association removed homosexuality from its list of mental disorders, but it was as recently as November 2011 that the British Psychoanalytic Council issued its "position statement" on homosexuality, which said "it does not accept that a homosexual orientation is evidence of a disturbance of the mind or in development".

Five of the nine lines of the statement provide an assurance that candidates for their training programmes will not be discriminated against on the grounds of sexuality. It was a curious emphasis, as such discrimination was already unlawful in the UK.

The necessity of issuing the statement reflected a concern about the decreasing numbers of applicants to train in organisations that pursued a certain tradition of Freudian thought that could be said to have its origins in Jung's distancing psychoanalysis from the arguments of the *Three Essays* (1905d), the debates over the nature of feminine sexuality that took place between Freud, Freudians, and their opponent contemporaries in the 1920s and 30s, and the later developments of what might be loosely termed the British and American schools. These post-Freudian currents took issue with Freud, based on their clinical researches, converting Freud's theory of the libido into a looser model of psychical energy, giving emphasis to the effects of biology and anatomy, and equating psychic development with heterosexuality respectively. This had the effect of "pathologising" homosexuality, associating it with perversion and psychosis, resulting in a "widespread psychoanalytic endorsement of heterosexuality as biologically ordained, natural, fitting, mature, the essence of human sexuality and relationships" (Ryan, 2000, p. 313)—"pathology" being read within these currents of psychoanalysis as the study of illness, of disorders, and of disease rather than giving emphasis to its etymological roots as *pathos* (πάθος), meaning "experience" or "suffering", and—*logia* (-λογία), "an account of". This, in turn, had its effects, which include an adversarial relationship between queer scholars and psychoanalysis; a reluctance, fear, or antipathy of homosexuals to enter psychoanalytic work; and a prohibition against the training of homosexuals as psychoanalysts.

Thus the relationship between queer and psychoanalysis is a complex one, with some queer theorists and activists taking the view that psychoanalysis is integral to the discourse of heteronormativity and others finding within it a potentiality for resistance to social processes of normalisation, and to thinking about sex and love.

Those writing under the banner "queer theory" take up the questions and concerns of the hysteric. Queer theory foregrounds questions of sexual difference, the body, desire, sexuality, and enjoyment. And just as hysteria is thought to have disappeared by some commentators, and yet keeps re-emerging in different forms, Merck (2005, p. 87) has drawn attention to the fact that it is already customary to predict the demise of queer theory, although this demise is always postponed.

Queer theory emerged, in part, in response to a feminism. Teresa de Lauretis, Eve Sedgwick, and Judith Butler—who, arguably, set the intellectual agenda and conceptual groundwork for queer theory in the 1990s—were motivated by a concern to maintain lesbian experience against the tendency for it to disappear into the category of "woman".

Queer theory coalesced out of a growing sense—among feminists, sexual minorities, and marginalised others—that constructions of identity and political strategies were based on a notion of unification by way of a problematic categorisation. Queer theory aims, according to de Lauretis (who is frequently credited with first coining the term) at transgressing and transcending "the terms lesbian and gay to designate distinct kinds of life-styles, sexualities, sexual practices, communities, issues, publications and discourses [...] to produce another discursive horizon, another way of thinking the sexual" (de Lauretis, 1991, p. iv). The history of hysteria can also be read as a particularly feminine questioning and protest, a subversion of an established order through a radical questioning of sex, sexuality, and desire, and its outcome was another way of thinking the sexual—psychoanalysis. Freud's Dora, for example, and his young female homosexual (1920) who both, in their different ways, subverted and frustrated their physicians/fathers, and whose homosexual desires can be seen as an attempt to transcend, or at least refuse, the limits of their sexed position. Of course, this is the very argument of second-wave feminists, who claim the hysterics of psychoanalysis as their own, a point not lost on Freud (1920, p. 169). So is queer saying anything different? Feminism could be said to interrogate the category woman, but nevertheless reduces it to one. Queer on the other hand questions and undermines the very notion of sexed differentiation.

For psychoanalysis, masculinity and femininity are symbolic positions, the only positions available to the human subject. And, it is the limit of these two possible subjective positions that both queer theory and hysteria attempt to address and problematise.

Queer: a new site of hysteria

The young woman with the diagnosis of *globus hystericus*—a lump in her throat that had been there since being told of the death of her baby brother—did not follow her lover with the prestigious job. Instead, she turned into a "boi". The term has many uses. It is used to refer to the passive partner in S/M sexual relationships, or to the woman who is transitioning to a man—whether with surgery or hormone treatment—or to the younger partner or, indeed, the one who identifies as younger. In this case, s/he rejected both the trappings of femininity, "girly-things", as she described them, and those s/he took as masculine—responsibilities of a career, of owning a car. S/he told her analyst that she had never wanted to grow up and that boys—and bois—have all the fun. The analyst, taking her lead from Freud (1920, p. 169) interpreted this wish not to grow up as a narcissistic defence against "bodily disfigurement connected" with pregnancy (ibid.). Her analysand laughingly retorted that she had become a lesbian because sex, at least sex with a man, was disgusting to her. Furthermore, in this case, the analyst was alert to her analysand's wish not to grow up and the identification with her brother, who would never grow up. While female homosexuality has always been associated with masculinity, with lesbians throughout history adopting masculine styles of dress, the queer category of boi is more fluid, and indicates nothing about sexual practice. The advent of queer and its project of undermining and destabilising heteronormative relations, has resulted in a myriad of new identity categories that the hysteric might occupy. Freud's homosexual girl had only the option of turning into a man (ibid., p. 158), while today's hysteric has many other options. Taking up the position of boi proved a useful place in which this hysteric's inherent bisexuality could find expression and did not so much provide an answer to the question of sexed subjectivity, but provided a place for its further interrogation.

But perhaps what this fictional clinical case best illustrates is that desire follows a logic all its own. Nobody can really make rational sense of why they like whatever it is they like, and queer provides a site for the articulation and protest of hysteria today.

Notes

1. See for an example of one summary, Akagi and House, 2002.
2. For an elaboration of this argument see for example Borossa, 2001, p. 72; White, 2006, pp. 126–129. 108; Verhaeghe, 2004, p. 365.

References

Abbott, M. (2014). *The Fever*. London: Picador.
Akagi, H., & House, A. (2002). The clinical epidemiology of hysteria: Vanishingly rare or just vanishing? *Psychological Medicine, 32*: 191–194.
Appignanesi, L. (2008). *Mad, Bad and Sad: A History of Women and the Mind Doctors from 1800 to the Present*. London, Virago, 2009.

Austin, J. L. (1975). *How to Do Things with Words*. Cambridge, MA: Harvard University Press.
Bollas, C. (2000). *Hysteria*. London: Routledge.
Borossa, J. (2001). *Hysteria*. Duxford, Icon Books.
Butler, J. (1990). *Gender Trouble*. London: Routledge, 1999.
Butler, J. (1993). *Bodies That Matter: On the Discursive Limits of "Sex"*. New York: Routledge.
Butler, J. (1997). *The Psychic Life of Power: Theories in Subjection*. New York: Routledge.
De Lauretis, T. (1991). Queer theory: lesbian and gay sexualities: an introduction. *Differences*, 3: iii–xviii.
Freud, S. (1905d). *Three Essays on the Theory of Sexuality. S. E., 7*. London: Hogarth.
Freud, S. (1905e). Fragment of an analysis of a case of hysteria. *S. E., 7*. London: Hogarth.
Freud, S. (1917). Mourning and melancholia. *S. E., 14*. London: Hogarth.
Freud, S. (1920). The psychogenesis of a case of homosexuality in a woman. *S. E., 18*. London: Hogarth.
Freud, S. (1923). *The Ego and the Id. S. E., 19*. London: Hogarth.
Foucault, M. (1976). *The History of Sexuality, Vol. 1, An Introduction* (Trans. R. Hurley). New York: Pantheon, 1978.
Gherovici, P. (2010). *Please Select Your Gender: From the Invention of Hysteria to the Democratizing of Transgenderism*. New York: Routledge.
Grosz, E. (1994). *Experimental Desire: Rethinking Queer Subjectivity*. In: J. Copjec (Ed.), Supposing the Subject (pp. 133–158). London: Verso.
Harris, M. B., Deary, L. J., Wilson, J. A. (1996). Life events and difficulties in relation to the onset of globus pharynges. *Journal of Psychosomatic Research, 40*: 603–615.
Hennessy, R. (2000). *Profit and Pleasure*. New York: Routledge.
Lacan, J. (1993). *The Seminar. Book III. The Psychoses, 1955–56*. (Trans. R. Grigg). London: Routledge.
Laplanche, J., & Pontalis, J. -B. (1973). *The Language of Psychoanalysis*. London: Karnac, 1988.
Merck, M. (2005). Afterword. In: I. Morland & A Wilcox (Eds.), *Queer Theory* (pp. 187–191) London: Palgrave Macmillan.
Mitchell, J. (2000). *Mad Men and Medusas*. London: Allen Lane.
Moncayo, R. (2008). *Evolving Lacanian Perspectives for Clinical Practice*. London: Karnac.
Ryan, J. (2000). Can psychoanalysis understand homophobia: Resistance in the clinic. In: T. Dean & C. Lane (Eds.), *Homosexuality & Psychoanalysis* (pp. 307–321) London: UCP.
Salih, S. (2002). *Judith Butler*. London: Routledge.

Sinfield, A. (2005). *Cultural Politics—Queer Reading*. London: Routledge.
Turner, W. (2000). *A Genealogy of Queer Theory*. Philadelphia: Temple University Press.
Verhaeghe, P. (2004). *On Being Normal and Other Disorders: A Manual for Clinical Psychodiagnostics*. New York: Other Press.
White, J. (2006). *Generation: Preoccupations and Conflicts in Contemporary Psychoanalysis*. London: Routledge.

CHAPTER FOUR

Necessity and seduction: a section of hysteria

Vincent Dachy

Onset

From Antiquity through the Middle Ages the conceptions of hysteria ranged from "uterine migration" to "diabolic possession". The anatomical investigations of the Renaissance inaugurated paths towards "modern medicine", which contributed to the formation of psychiatry and, famously in the case of hysteria, to Charcot. Then came Freud, whose place in this hystory remains distinct. But, for some sixty years or so in more recent history, diagnostic manuals of mental disorders have gradually whittled down hysteria, as a category, leaving it in the depot of history, only to keep the symptom of conversion in their arsenal. Do some people want hysteria to disappear? Do some people object to the name itself: far too sexist and rooted in bygone superstitions not to be rendered obsolete? Or has hysteria simply disappeared? After all, everybody knows the predilection of hysteria for the figure of the Father and, if it is true that this figure has been dwindling for a century or two, perhaps hysteria has finally faded away accordingly?

Analytic derivations

One could easily argue that everything has been said about hysteria, everything and its contrary also. But throughout it all we can still distinguish the puzzlement vis-à-vis "body manifestations" on the one hand, from the perplexed stupefaction in front of "over the top" displays of affects, on the other.

Symptom and simulation

The distinction between manifestations through im-pressions in the body and manifestations through "over the top" ex-pressions (which, presumably, led to the common use of the word "hysterical") does not obstruct the converging suggestions of simulation, exaggeration, or inauthenticity to characterise hysteria. Is hysteria a sham, an unfortunate comedy of errors, a devious manipulation? Freud underlined a very strong diagnostic criterion for the hysteric symptom of conversion: it does not follow the laws of physiology. This observation is still crucial in medicine today, in neurology, for instance. But, of course, some eagerly claim that not everything is known in the realm of physiology. The exaggeration[1] of expression, similarly, caught Freud's attention. It did not seem to follow the usual rules of reactive proportionality. Here again, an excess seemed to display and indicate that something else was at stake, something "under the top", something "transposed".

Transfer and expression

Could it be that in both instances something apparently "fake", "pseudo", was manifesting something true? Freud's cardinal contribution on hysteria was to elicit just that: a truth is manifested by way of a detour, via its incarnation in the body (embodied im-pression) or through its voiced/exhibited embodiment, words, or gestures (embodied ex-pression), giving it its "theatrical" aspect too often associated for the observer with a dismissive sentiment of "this is not for real."

Freud also discovered that this "piece of truth" was transposed following routes furrowed by language. These symptoms were pressing signs that kept a more or less obvious link with the (subjective) truth, with the truth-value they were manifesting. Freud called these transformations "condensation" and "displacement" and Jacques Lacan gave them linguistic equivalents: "metaphor" and "metonymy" (as functions of meaning production). It was therefore possible that a truth-value be manifested unbeknownst to the speaking-being expressing it. As it has become known, this particular operation is called "repression" and it lies on the hypothesis called the "unconscious".

But what is the truth in question?

Shock

This is the other and arguably most fundamental discovery of psychoanalysis: the truth in question ensued an encounter with sexuality.[2] It is a crucial real(ity) of clinical praxis to discern that there is no automatic entrance, admission, for "human beings" into language or into sexuality (despite, or as a result of, all the genetic wiring that one can suppose or/and demonstrate). Both have to be encountered and both encounters are subject to incidents, to contingencies.

In the singular encounter with the real of sexuality lies the truth to which the hysteric symptom attests. So the truth in question actually bears witness to a real.

Seduction

At first Freud thought that a child had been prematurely seduced into sexual adventure—against her will, or not. Then he realised that the seduction did not have to be the direct result of some malevolent deed but was mainly linked to a (traumatic) experience, the result of which was the realisation of the existence (ek-sistence) of sexuality, and, therefore, of femininity and masculinity. Not that this distinction between deed and thought should make no difference socially or legally, but, unconsciously, what mattered was the specific encounter a speaking being had with a disruptive excitement that she couldn't tolerate or accept. The encounter was suffered, not taken on and up. The event involved an arousal through an imposed encounter with the Other's desire: an imposed seduction.[3] "Nothing to do with me", the subject may profess, but, still, it left a trace, a mark. After all, not every unpleasant experience leaves a mark; often we simply step aside, move away, and are left with nothing but indifference, not even a memory or an impression. Not in this instance however; the mark remains invested, gets re-invested just after the "event" or quite a while later. "*Nachträglichkeit*" of investment. The experience occurs and may be suffered indeed but it concerns, interests[4] the subject—at the time of the event or retrospectively. An event becomes important whenever it becomes significant. It is determinant that albeit "unacceptable", unbearable even, the event is, becomes, significant. The subject is surprised, shocked, imposed upon but arrested (and here we find the subjective implication—not to be confused with a "liking") albeit unpleasantly, insufferably so; let us say, disruptively so.

How will a speaking being respond to the problem of sexuality encountered through the disruptive desire of the Other?[5] This, mainly, means to know how to find a "know-how" to integrate what one "feels" (from affects to sensations and back again) with what one thinks (the domain of fantasies, so much wider than that of reason), and vice versa. What does constitute the hysteric arrangement?

Arrangement (positioning, defence, modus vivendi)

The response of the subject, which is mainly what constitutes a subjective position(ing), operates in a twofold manner, at the levels of "feeling" and "meaning", in order to find a bearable arrangement with the unacceptable contingency.

1. To transpose the singularity of the significant experience in the body. An unacceptable, unexpected, not experienced before or unfathomable, body-sensation becoming an affect as a result of the significance it is given, is drained away, reduced to a sensation detached from its sexual significance (i.e., reduced to a "straightforward" bodily manifestation, a tensing perhaps, which is then often addressed to medicine).
2. To transpose the singularity of the significant experience by insinuating it in discourse. To "dis-affect" the sexual actuality of the "It should not have happened" (which accompanies the trauma) by demanding satisfaction for an offence, attributing it to a flaw in the (power of the) Other—potency of which the subject thereby makes herself the more or less dedicated champion. The shock of the event, which shattered or fractured a belief that the subject had enjoyed until then (or a belief that is constituted retrospectively as a means to "make sense" of what happened), is imputed to a fault of the (idealised and supposed) instance of (expected) satisfaction,

that is, the instance which guarantees that "Things are what they should be".[6] Let us call it Father Christmas, for instance. Not Mother Christmas so much, as it tends to operate more as the figure of Love/Care rather than as the figure of Desiring.

In the realm of love, nevertheless

In the hysteric arrangement the effort is made to keep and maintain the traumatic encounter with an enjoyment that poses the question of desiring, within the realm of love (and frequently one can observe a pressing confusion: Does X desire or love me? Do I love or desire X?[7] The love in question is not mainly love for the occasional "(ir)responsible perpetrator" or perpetration—although that is not excluded—but for the conservation of the frame of love in relation to the Other. Such a frame helps to determine the problem of femininity (and masculinity) which haunts the hysterical subject since s/he has, one day, encountered the contingency of sexuality and the indeterminacy that accompanies it. The hysterical arrangement aims at keeping the relation to the imposition of enjoyment within the frame of love sustained by a (symbolic) Order.

An ordinary occurrence of this attempted arrangement is the following: the encounter with the disruptive enjoyment elicits the sensitivity to the question of the "object" that causes desiring. But the subject doesn't want to be desired as an object (for, or because of, "my body", "my looks", "my money", "my status", etc.) but wants to be desired as and for "oneself", that is, wants to be desired for the same reasons as those of being loved—but still wants to feel desired sexually. What a puzzle to realize that enjoyment, love, and desire do not constitute a simple and automatic, "natural" continuum! As the traumatic disruptive enjoyment[8] is too much to deal with, love (and its idealisation) is called for to make it passable. Love attenuates the shock of the traumatism, gives it a limit. By seeking the protection of the powers of love (which keep separate enjoyment and desire—I desire you but because I love you I will not enjoy you … just as yet) desiring can be upheld as un-realised, and the re-encounter of the problematic enjoyment kept at bay. And a surplus-enjoyment of causing desire can be derived from the operation, an enjoyment of seduction, for example.

The difficulty for the subject is to grasp her implication in this arrangement and the impossibility behind the failure of potency (which is never too difficult to discover) ascribed to the Other. Whatever the contingency of its encounter (which is not indifferent, however) there is always an impossibility at the core of sexuality: the impossibility of a "resolving principle of due satisfaction" (see Lacan's moto "There is no sexual relation").

Necessity versus contingency

The Other's desire puts in question the expectation of Satisfaction (i.e., "the satisfaction that should be") and the Necessity of love (inasmuch as love transforms the contingency of an encounter into a necessity of being—"We were made for each other", "You are my child", etc.—and therefore makes separations painful but the variations and inconstancies of desiring also. Who or what is desired?

How do enjoyment, love, and desire, clash or match, join or jar? The flesh, as site, "*situs*", locus of enjoyment, (which, as everybody knows, is weak), love, as what gives value to being (without which life may feel quite lonely), detached from sexual satisfaction, and desiring, as want-to[-enjoy]-being, (which sustains the feeling of being alive), do not always dance hand in hand. This shaky dance which is inevitably foisted on speaking beings, does not reach an automatic solution or a euphonic balance. There is no necessity operating automatically to solve this quandary. Hysteria is one of the attempts to sustain the supposition of such necessity. Not the necessity often attributed in perversion to "nature", "instincts", and their "a-subjectivity"[9] but the necessity that there should be an order, an authority, a master which supports, ensures, the resolution of the discontinuity between enjoyment, love, and desire. Antigones, "witches", "martyrs", and other upholders of the laws of the skies, but their triplet sisters also, the *belles âmes*, paragons of all kinds of puritanisms, and the sirens, irresistible seductresses, provocative and charming, all so influential in civilisation inasmuch as they devote themselves to the dimension of truth, even if they seldom know where their passion is rooted. Champions of the purism of desiring within the pasture of love.[10]

Outcome

We may observe that the father as figure of authority, guarantor of order, security, fairness, justice, etc., has somewhat faded in some provinces nowadays. Disappeared? No, multiplied or diffused rather. There may very well not be a unique figure able to inspire overall respect and authority anymore but should such a mastery figure appear we can reckon that it would soon be challenged by science, lawyers, and hysterics (unless the latter choose to support him passionately!). Yet, beyond the "classical" figures can we not descry figures of "contemporary hysteria" addressing themselves to medicine, to law, to science, to politics without forgetting religion?

Consider, for example, how much the question of "abuse" has grown and spread in recent decades. In front of the figures of power/mastery, which press on towards satisfaction with a cynical grip and very few, if any, lawful premises, whistle-blowers have arisen.[11] In that respect, the demanding figure of the victim gives us a pretty good idea of the diffusion of hysteria. The victim, as figure of discourse and enjoyment,[12] which responds to the masters of exploitation and abuse, as personifications of "what it should not be like", calls their enjoyment into question. And the ignorance of their own does not make their unveilings, claims, or protestations (silent or vocal) less pertinent.

Envoi

Should we keep the word "hysteria"? Tongues have evolved, and will evolve, with discourses trying to find "new ways" of grasping, circumscribing, and taming the persistent and interminable real of (dis)satisfaction.

Should we discard the category, the concept? That is more dangerous for our intelligence, but concepts, in psychoanalysis if nowhere else, are always as good as the use we have of them.

What should not disappear, though, is the consideration of the symptomatic arrangements and "constructive solutions", speaking beings find about (dis)satisfaction, particularly when it comes to the thorny problem of enjoyment. What has been called hysteria is one of the most vocal and expressive advocate of this problem in the "social field", one of the symptoms and one of the discourses that have been confronting our social bond(s) with the dimension of truth. Who wants to do without that?

At least the answer to this question is known.

60   HYSTERIA TODAY

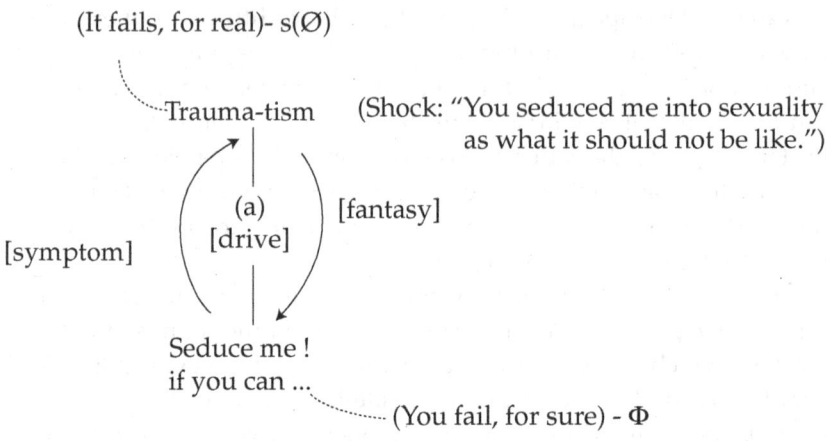

A schema.

Notes

1. The word originally meant "pile up", "accumulate", later "intensify praise or blame", "dwell on a virtue or fault", giving rise to current senses. This etymology is strikingly apt. We should add that "exaggeration" applies as both "too much" and "too little", convulsions or screaming but also paralysis, numbness, or indifference, for example.
2. By the notion of enjoyment ("jouissance" in French, introduced, as a concept in psychoanalysis, by J. Lacan) we understand whatever concerns the dimension of excitements invested for themselves; "sexuality", in its broadest meaning—not only related to sexual intercourse even if it has an elective importance—concentrates the investment of excitements through the real(ity) of being sexuated.
3. From Latin "seducere", from se—"away, apart" + ducere "to lead." "To be led away, astray"; led to know something that one would have preferred not to experience/know. We should underline the fact that the encounter may also occur as an absence of expected satisfaction, "not being desired" for instance, a disappointment which amounts easily to a reproach to the "misleading Other".
4. From Latin "interesse": "differ, be important," from inter—"between" + esse "be." The—t was added partly by association with Old French interest, "damage, loss", apparently from Latin interest, "it is important". The original sense was "the possession of a share in or a right to something".

5. This indicates that whatever the modalities of encounter with sexuality may be, through the Other's desire as in this case, or else, every speaking-being will have to find a "know-some-how" with sexuality.
6. 1/ Shock—sensation—S(Ø)—signifier—affect—sensation—Φ 2/ -φ/Φ.
   This second operation has been particularly well highlighted by J. Lacan in a way that has clarified the dignity of hysteria. See Seminars 5 (chap. 22, 26), 8 (chap. 17 especially), and 17 (chap. 6, 8, 12), for instance.
7. The differentiation between enjoyment and love is not stable in psychosis; the differentiation between enjoyment and desire is obfuscated in perversion.
8. "Enjoyment" here, following Lacan's conceptualisation of "jouissance", is pointing—contrary to a common and "pleasant" use of the term—to an in-sistence in the field of satisfaction, which relentlessly calls for "more", which "urges on" regardless of common sense, decency, reputation, and, actually, ignores what we generally call pleasure itself. "Enjoyment" as the radical dimension of satisfaction that doesn't necessarily stop at the threshold of pain. The well-thinking, clean-living, sanctimonious people of good repute will simply call these manifestations "abnormal", "disorders", or, more charitably, "excesses", but only to ignore that this dimension of satisfaction belongs to anybody's life albeit in very variable ways and degrees, some far more absorbing or disturbing than others for someone's life or for morality.
9. What we call "perversion" as an analytic category/register—with the judgmental connotations that this carries, could also be reconsidered as such a "subjective arrangement" that is, a particular response to the subjection that the traumatisms of language and sexuality impose on the living-speaking-being.
10. "Impurity" or the impossible purity of desiring is more the problem of obsessional neurosis. One could read the "The House with the Mezzanine" by A. Chekhov and delight in one enlightening contrast drawn between hysteria and obsessionality.
11. Since there is not an unique consistent figure of order any more (i.e., no figure drawing an internal principled limit to enjoyment; often too comfortably reduced to "patriarchy"), entrepreneurs, speculators, dealers, and other traders are often depicted as the mastery figures of today, ducking and diving external limitations, mostly or only preoccupied by the best "return". It still remains for anthropologists, historians, and the kind to show whether the fading of the figure of the father has rendered the commerce of enjoyment more conspicuous or whether the makeup of this commerce has indeed changed with the dwindling of the figures

of principled authority and the rise of figures of management of excesses instead.

12. Let us distinguish the individual victim of some dreadful wrongdoing (more so than the individual victim of an unlucky strike of chance) from the individual's endorsement of the identification to the "victim" which then becomes a positioning of the subject. And let us also insist that such endorsement can be just as remarkable, socially useful, and fruitful and that it can become an endless attachment to the offence itself.

CHAPTER FIVE

Fifty shades of literary success: the vampire's appeal

Geneviève Morel

Translated by Kristina Valendinova

Fifty Shades of Grey, written by British author E. L. James (2011) and quickly followed by two sequels, *Fifty Shades Darker* and *Fifty Shades Freed*, was first published in New York in April 2012. Usually seen as part of the "erotic romance" genre, it sold one million copies more quickly than any other book in the history of publishing, outselling both *The Da Vinci Code* and the *Harry Potter* series, and beating all other records in terms of both the number of copies sold and the rapidity of sales.[1] So far, it has sold seventy million copies worldwide. However, despite its commercial triumph, *Fifty Shades* has also been tremendously controversial, as shown by the split reviews on online booksellers' websites. Moreover, with rare exceptions, most critics have found it "poorly written", "tedious", "deserving of the name 'grey' but completely lacking in 'shades'", "implausible", "soppy", "insipid or corny", full of platitudes and clichés, of banal eroticism, and so on and so forth.

It is quite clear that literary critics are out of tune with the majority of the book's audience: although it has been ridiculed as "mommy porn", there is no question of its phenomenal success with female readers—who, moreover, are not necessarily stay-at-home mothers, but are likely to be young, educated women with a good level of income.[2] If we are to believe online comments, the novel has also given some of its women readers the opportunity to change their sexual practices and embrace BDSM[3]—besides, it has led to a boom in the sales of sex toys, the use of which it teaches in the tone of a beginner's manual.

The sociological approach

According to the Israeli sociologist Eva Illouz,[4] who has recently published a book on feminine love (2012), the success of *Fifty Shades*, unparalleled within its literary genre,[5] cannot be explained solely by its being a kind of "S&M manual", but rather it has to do with the traditional gender roles of patriarchal society—the submissive female versus the triumphant male—which the story conceals beneath the fashionable practices of soft BDSM. We could of course immediately object that *Fifty Shades* is not the first erotic novel with S&M themes, indeed that it has had many famous predecessors: leaving aside such classics as the work of Sade or Sacher-Masoch, we might for example think of the 1954 French novel *The Story of O* or, more recently, *Beasts* by the American writer Joyce Carol Oates.[6] But one could also argue that these books are of a completely different nature—more brutal and tragic—and that they were written for a different, more sophisticated and literary readership. In this sense they are not, properly speaking, "erotic romance stories" because they lack the obligatory happy ending, where a straight couple that has overcome a number of obstacles eventually attains marital bliss. Illouz argues that *Fifty Shades* should instead be seen as a kind of female *Bildungsroman* or a conduct novel (because it is British)—seemingly subversive, but in fact quite normative. It is in this sense that we should understand, first, the way in which the novel's heroine Ana constantly refers to *Tess of the d'Urbervilles*, her favourite novel, as a fascinating story of love, but also an example not to be followed; and, second, her (short-lived) revolt against her S&M lover Christian Grey. Illouz stresses that *Fifty Shades* gives both protagonists a role in the male-female relationship, which has been greatly destabilised by late capitalism. The new market economy, as well as the scientific and social transformations it entails, allows women to have children without men, demands less self-control from men, and removes the need for traditional family structures. We supposedly live in chaotic times, where traditional sexual roles and criteria of sexual identity have become insufficient. According to Illouz, S&M would thus provide a novel solution to the difficulties of a sexually uncertain era.

It is true that, because there is nothing natural about becoming a man or a woman, we all wait for some knowledge about sex, first from our parents—a hope that is usually disappointed—and then from society at large, and what it can transmit to us through culture. As Lacan says: "On the side of the Other [...] *order and norms* must be instituted which tell the subject *what a man or a woman must do*"[7] (2006a, p. 720). That is, of course, the case, but this lack of knowledge about sex, which is so keenly felt and which we hear about from many of our analysands, is a universal problem. We have no reason to think that it is more of an issue today than it was in the past, unless we fall prey to a common prejudice, one that usually goes hand in hand with a hint of melancholic nostalgia: namely, that we are living in a "decadent era" and previous generations had it all organised much better. Here, we may recall Lacan's ironic mention, in relation to Longus' romance *Daphnis and Chloe*, of the figure of the old woman who is supposed to teach a young innocent couple how to make love. Of course nobody needs a manual to discover the erotic effects of spanking—if we have forgotten our own childhood, we need only to reread Rousseau's *Confessions* or observe the sexual play-fighting that typically occurs between pre-teens.

The sociological approach, which explains the dazzling success of *Fifty Shades* by the fact that it is a kind of coming-of-age story, therefore seems lacking. Shouldn't we instead think that its popularity stems not so much from its usefulness as a manual on "how to improve sex with your regular partner", but rather from the simple fact that reading it produces a special kind of pleasure? More accounts point in this latter direction.[8]

Hysterical trance on the London underground

It seems that many women, especially in London, have read the novel discreetly as an e-book on their daily commute, in a kind of shared solitude that reminds us of the hysterical epidemic which Freud described, in quite a different context, at the beginning of the twentieth century. Recall the scene from a girls' boarding school: one of the students receives a letter from her lover, which arouses her jealousy, and she has a hysterical fit (Freud, 1921, p. 106). Then some of the other girls start having fits too. As Freud stresses, they do not do so out of sympathy, as common sense would have it, but because they identify with their friend. They too would like to have a secret lover, even if it meant suffering. In order to obtain a lover, in their fantasy at least, they accept the disagreeable consequence—jealousy—by a kind of reverse causality: in advance, as it were, as a proof of his existence. This triggers the collective hysterical crisis. Hysterical identification, Lacan argues, is a structure based "on lack taken as an object, rather than on its cause" (2001, p. 557). These young girls are in fact not connected to one another in any way, except for none of them having a lover. The collective hysterical crisis therefore tells us nothing about the singular fantasy that would allow each of them to find a suitable lover. The hysterical crisis is essentially a mode of symptomatic sexual satisfaction, which simultaneously allows the subject a double gain—to make do without a real partner, and avoid all knowledge about "the cause of lack," that is, about the cause of one's desire, which remains unconscious. Knowing something about one's own unconscious desire in fact requires a courage that the neurotic usually struggles to find.

Does *Fifty Shades* bring us back to the Freudian boarding school? Are we witnessing a global hysterical trance fostered by a certain kind of modern-day solitude, where millions of female readers are using a vaguely erotic romantic novel (only thirteen per cent of the scenes in the first volume of the trilogy involve sex and still fewer in the sequels) to "enjoy themselves" on their way back from work? If this were so, for some of them it would mean absolutely nothing in terms of trying something new with their real-life partners. On the contrary, it would allow them to continue doing without, in exchange for a phantasmatic pleasure—which is perfectly in line with a certain rejection of men that is inherent to the hysterical structure, as we have known since Freud's Dora case.

Although the argument seems convincing, it doesn't quite satisfy us because it leaves obscure the exact cause of the collective craze: why has this particular novel been so successful, rather than any other? We have mentioned its conventional and monotonous style, but let us return to its plot. Contrary to how it is usually described, E. L. James claims to have written a love story, rather than a story about sex.[9] The S&M-themed scenes only bring sexual enjoyment to Ana, a young anorexic virgin, against her will (and they do so very unconvincingly—she climaxes as soon as her lover touches her). What she really wants is not this kind of pleasure, but a story of love and sex ending in marriage and children (and that is also the very conventional ending of the whole trilogy). What really drives the plot is something else: namely, that the heroine gets to "fix" the hero, a broken man—which is completely in line with hysteria. Before being adopted by an ideal family, Christian had in fact suffered severe child abuse, and his proclivity for S&M is its unfortunate consequence. His mother, a prostitute,[10] abandoned him to the cruelty of her pimp. As an adult man, he cannot stand tenderness and prefers to interpose between his own body and that of his partner a whole maze of cords and an arsenal of tools, in order to keep her at a distance. However, the beautiful Ana manages to bring him round and show him who the real master is. The trilogy therefore demonstrates how a young and fragile but determined woman can, by becoming the cause of a man's desire and provoking his love, accomplish the miracle of cure, while reducing the slightly too *hardcore* part of the machinery required by her lover to just a few gadgets that could increase her own pleasure. The initiation is reciprocal: her lover teaches her about sex and in return he learns from her about love. Ultimately, this well-balanced combination of sentimental romance and passionate sex stages the story of a woman's submission only to show how she can in fact dominate her partner and make him serve her own pleasure. This is perfectly compatible with the hysteric's desire to be the real master—a desire that E. L. James has successfully echoed among her female readers. *Fifty Shades* is thus a vibrant tribute to a successful hysteria.

The generalised hysterical trance around *Fifty Shades* would therefore derive from, first, the solitary jouissance of the shared erotic lack, second, the desire to be the master of the male master, and third, the desire to "fix" a castrated man—three familiar topoi of hysteria, which are founded on a structural relationship to castration.

However, if we are happy with this explanation, are we not ourselves behaving like the young girls at Freud's boarding school or the female readers of *Fifty Shades*, that is, avoiding the cause of desire that is at work in the collective hysterical trance? The cause of desire, the cause of lack, is in fact to be found in the fantasy of each female subject; it cannot be mistaken for the shared erotic lack that produces both the identification and the trance. There must be something else at play in the book's success, something other than the mechanisms of lack and privation. A book that speaks to women so deeply must have touched, by some of its qualities, the "cause of desire"[11] at work in their own fantasy—and it remains for us to decipher how.

Fifty Shades and *Twilight:* The transference from vampires to S&M

Let's return to where *Fifty Shades* first began. Its author, the former TV executive E. L. James, wrote fanfiction under the pen name "Snowqueens Icedragon" for several blogs, based on the highly popular vampire saga *Twilight*, the first volume of which came out in 2005. Because her episodes were considered too risqué for the *Twilight* universe, she was eventually banned from posting on these sites. She then rewrote the stories and reposted them on her own website *Fiftyshades.com* as original fiction, resulting in the first online publication of the romance under the title *Master of the Universe*. Its heroes were originally Bella and Edward, the protagonists of *Twilight*.[12]

Fifty Shades is more than inspired by *Twilight*—in many ways it is an imitation. This, however, has not prompted any complaints from Stephenie Meyer, Twilight's author and a committed Mormon, who prefers to dispel in the minds of her readers any suspicion of similarities between James's explosive book and her own chaste story, usually filed under the genre of Young Adult Romance (and sometimes ironically described as "abstinence porn").[13] Meyer considers *Fifty Shades* a piece of smut, while the purity of her *Twilight* series supposedly derives from the unselfish nature of true love that she has herself experienced. *Twilight* is a kind of fictionalised autobiography. Meyer allegedly wrote it after a vivid dream of an amazingly beautiful couple, which she had the night after the birth of her third child. Inspired by the dream and as if in an ecstatic trance, she then wrote day and night—only stopping to feed the baby—in a kind of fit of automatic writing.[14] The chaste relationship between the heroes of *Twilight* is dictated by Edward's nature. While Bella is a seventeen-year-old human girl, Edward is a 108-year-old vampire, eternally frozen at the age of eighteen. He is torn between his love for Bella, which is a new and strange feeling for him, and a compulsive desire, quite normal for a vampire, to devour her. He is therefore struggling not to touch her, while the imposed abstinence makes Bella's desire reach a burning point. Their relationship, oscillating between temptation and restraint, resembles courtly love. They only start having sex after marriage, in the fourth volume called *Breaking Dawn* (Meyer, 2010, pp. 78–89). Although these scenes are not described directly, they are apparently very violent, leaving Bella covered in bruises because of Edward's superhuman strength. On their wedding night, Bella gets pregnant with a half-human, half-vampire child. The little girl puts her mother's life at risk by drinking her blood and devouring her from the inside. This is not only a transposition of an autobiographical trait—Meyer experienced her first pregnancy as a vampire's attack—but also a feeling we commonly find in the clinic. In order to save her and their daughter from a certain death, Edward is forced to bite Bella, with her consent. By injecting her with his "venom" he transforms her into a vampire, something he had previously always refused to do. He himself is in fact living unhappily as a "vegetarian vampire" (a strange oxymoron which means that he only eats animal and not human flesh, at the expense of a painful and eternal asceticism) and would have preferred Bella to preserve her human fragility.

We can see the parallels between the two sagas, the *Fifty Shades* trilogy and *Twilight*, even in the details, which include, to give only a few examples:[15]

- The electric current that passes between the two lovers like a discharge every time they touch (James, 2011, pp. 8, 15, 27; Meyer, 2005, pp. 38, 61).
- On their first encounter, the heroine stumbles and the hero helps her stand up; (2011, p. 7; 2005, p. 20) he saves her from an accident or from an aggressive rival trying to rape or kill her; (2005, p. 47).
- The heroine is the daughter of divorced parents (2011, p. 46), has low self-esteem, and suffers from anorexia (2011, pp. 3–4, 75, 92; 2005, pp. 34, 184).
- She has a passion for literature (Thomas Hardy *vs.* Charlotte Bronte) (2011, p. 47; 2005, p. 33).
- The heroine's "inner goddess" (2011, pp. 67, 216), or the drive to jouissance (*pousse-au-jouir*); and, in the opposite direction, the "inner conscience" (2011, pp. 69, 94, 240) which holds Ana back, *vs.* Bella's discouraging or encouraging inner voice of the superego (2005, pp. 62, 220).
- The fact that both heroines, Ana and Bella, always get into trouble (2011, p. 48; 2005, p. 151).
- As for the hero, the eerie *vs.* perverse glow in his gaze, and his voice which makes his partner's heart melt (2011, pp. 15, 18, 224; 2005, p. 72); his ability to guess what others are thinking (2011, p. 224; 2005, p. 268).
- Both heroes were adopted by good parents and are trying to fight evil, for which they are not really responsible because it stems from their nature (a taste for S&M *vs.* the vampire's cannibalism) (2011, p. 154; 2005, p. 268).

- The heroes' need for control which protects, but also stifles, their partners; their physical brutality linked to previously suffered abuse *vs.* the vampire's supernatural force (2011, pp. 12, 282; 2005, p. 231).

  • The secondary characters (the best friend and the childhood friend who is desperately in love with the heroine) can also be put in parallel, as well as the existence of persecutors trying to "consume" the heroine metaphorically *vs.* literally (2011, pp. 39, 232; 2005, pp. 331–332). Some of the scenes in *Fifty Shades* are simply transposed from the supernatural world of vampires and prosaically adapted to the real world (for example, Grey takes Ana for a ride in his helicopter (2011, p. 89) or glider, while Edward flies over the forest, carrying Bella on his back (2005, p. 245)).

These small changes to the story are enough to make it appeal to a different readership, from teenagers to women of any age, because they perform a simple yet essential operation. This does not concern the main characters: deep down, Bella and Ana have remained very similar to each other—both adoring and desiring, worried about the Other's love and demand—and the same goes for the male heroes, two highly powerful men with superhuman abilities. The transformation only affects the latter's sexuality: Christian Grey's S&M "perversion", here explicitly genital, replaces Edward's vampirism, which is also a perversion (from the human perspective because it is quite natural for a vampire), but an oral one. Likewise, Grey's inner conflict and the way he must hold himself back in order not to lose Ana, who refuses to be his submissive, replaces the vampire's conflict between his amorous passion and his nature, which in this case he resolves by abstinence, in order not to lose Bella by killing her.

Is it not true that in the end, behind his S&M mask, Christian Grey remains a kind of vampire? And how might this explain the trilogy's immense success? To understand it, we must take another look at the vampire's essence.

Vampires are always "in"

What other creatures can boast such long-lasting acclaim as vampires, whose sparkling eyes, pointed ears, and sharp teeth have been popular since the Middle Ages, and who have only had to change their costumes and accessories over the centuries? Today, they are the topic of several highly popular television shows, but literature and the cinema have been keeping them alive for much longer, drawing on popular beliefs from the past. What is behind this continued interest? A number of contrasting hypotheses have been proposed by thinkers from different epistemological fields, but I shall only touch upon some of them briefly.

According to Claude Lecouteux, vampirism emerged from medieval beliefs, spreading as "a concern born from the breach of an order, from a split, shift or contradiction" (2009, p. 11) in the eighteenth century, the century of the Enlightenment. The decline of religion, together with scientific progress, caused this epidemic of irrationality. The devil survived the death of God by assuming the figure of the plaguing vampire. In parallel, the struggle against vampirism led by the Church replaced witch-hunts as early as the sixteenth century (Lecouteux, 2009, p. 138). Others have argued that the belief in vampires stems from epidemics of cholera or the plague, or even of rabies, because the disease was contracted through a bite. Yet other theorists—mostly positivists such as the French Benedictine monk Dom Calmet,[16] whose work, full of "tasty" anecdotes, inspired a number of writers (Lecouteux, 2009, p. 10)—speak about the malnutrition suffered by the Balkan peoples, which supposedly set their imaginations loose. Until the nineteenth century, rationalists thought that vampires were either the product of melancholic delusions or the fear of being buried alive in a state of catalepsy. Philosophically, and from a metaphysical perspective dating back to the Greeks, the blood craved by these creatures is a metaphor for life, or for the soul that triumphs over death. Still others see the never truly dead corpse which characterises the "non-dead" state of the vampire as the fundamental substrate of Christian resurrection (Gilbert, 2009) because on the Day of Judgment, the dead will re-emerge from the earth, as seen in the famous frescoes by Signorelli in Orvieto. The sheer number of hypotheses is the ultimate proof of the universal interest commanded by the "myth of the vampire" (Lecouteux, 2009, p. 15).

Voluptuous nightmares

"When a woman sleeps alone, the devil sleeps with her."[17]

The first psychoanalyst who became interested in vampires was Ernest Jones, in his work *On the Nightmare*, which he began writing in 1909. A nightmare is characterised by the sleeper's feelings of fear, suffocation, and helplessness. Because of its typically violent nature, Jones sees the nightmare as closer to a hallucination than a regular dream. Contrary to Freud, he believes that it is in all cases more pathological than normal. Assuming his thesis to have already been psychoanalytically verified, namely that "an attack of the Nightmare is an expression of a mental conflict over an incestuous desire," (Jones, 1931, p. 44) he now wishes to confirm its validity outside the field of psychoanalysis, by testing it on authors uninfluenced by psychological research. He relies in particular on the theories of the nineteenth-century mythologists, who "trace the belief in spirits to the experiences of the Nightmare" (Jones, 1931, p. 74). Some thinkers of previous centuries compared the sense of oppression on the chest and the accompanying dread, which are typical of nightmares, with being "crushed to the earth as beneath the weight of an enormous vampire" (Jones, 1931, p. 21). In the Middle Ages, one of the names for a nightmare was *incubus*—from the Latin name for the lustful demons that visit women at night in their dreams, seeking sexual enjoyment.

"It is as if an extraordinary lover envelops and penetrates you, loses himself in you. The enjoyment is enormous, but the nervous expenditure is terrible."[18] In English, the word nightmare indeed comes from "night mare"—a night demon.

Jones therefore embarks on a detailed study of different beliefs: in vampires, incubi, and other fantastic creatures such as werewolves, which are traditionally associated with nightmares and whose historical continuity has been proven by research.[19]

The oldest creatures in this series are the incubi, who are also the most likely to substantiate Jones's thesis of incestuous desire. Their nocturnal visits provoke half-erotic, half-nightmarish dreams, in which sex is barely concealed. Already in the seventeenth century, physicians saw them as "a product of voluptuous imagination," (Jones, 1931, p. 90) specifically of female imagination. The nineteenth-century French psychiatrists shared their opinion: "amorous illusions", "hysterical-religious" hallucinations, "erotomania", etc. The Church, on the other hand, was mostly interested in the extent to which the sleeper consented to and complied with the night visitor, and it judged women's religious guilt according to the degree to which their submission had been voluntary. During one exorcism, a priest noted that the young woman "seemed rather afraid of being saved" (Jones, 1931, p. 87). For Jones, the sleeper wards off the guilt associated with her incestuous desire for the father, by projecting it on to a demon that overpowers her against her will. Jones then distinguishes between two stages in human history: initially, the forbidden desire was projected on to an external demon, and then later on to internal and non-sexual bodily processes such as indigestion or the engorgement of the heart. The most important thing was that the subject denies her responsibility for the act committed in the dream. In this respect, the best method was to invoke something of an essentially religious nature, a divine night visitor rather than a malevolent one. Hence the ancient and officially approved method of *incubation*, which combined usefulness with pleasure by trying to cure sterility through a union with a god or with a departed being during sleep on his grave.

The historically later belief in vampires is also more complex because it combines the idea of death with that of sucking fresh blood and often disguises the sexual nature of the encounter with the vampire by various preliminary rituals of tenderness and love (kissing, caresses, seduction, etc.). While the incubus dreams have an overtly sexual, even obscene character, the vampire's visit is associated more closely with love. Vampires prefer to visit people they care about, especially those they were in love with while they were still alive. During the medieval epidemics of vampirism, a favourite method of detecting the cause was to make a widow admit that she had been visited by her recently departed spouse. Jones points out the similarities and continuity between the beliefs in incubi and vampires, which according to him have to do with female desire (Jones, 1931, pp. 126–127). In the case of vampires, the sexual guilt attached to incestuous desire would be projected on to the dead, again in order to free oneself of it. The belief in vampires is in fact a triple displacement of the incestuous wish: (1) love takes the form of an oral-sadistic impulse; (2) desire is transformed into fear; and (3) the incestuous father is replaced by a dead being. As for the idea of craving blood, it stems from the familiar equivalence between blood and sperm, thus revealing the repressed sexual character of the vampiric and cannibalistic act. Jones concludes that "the belief [in vampires] is, in fact, only an elaboration of that in the Incubus, and the essential elements of both are the same repressed desires and hatreds derived from early incest conflict."[20]

As we have seen, everyone from the Church to medical and psychiatric schools has agreed on the key role that feminine desire has played in the incredible survival of these beliefs throughout the centuries.

From incestuous desire to the "ideal incubus"

It is curious that, although he was a fine clinician of female sexuality, Jones did not choose to explore this path further and it was only Lacan who, having read his essay, made the connection between the incubus and feminine jouissance.

On the one hand, he emphasises the "key dimension" of the nightmare:

> The anxiety of the nightmare is experienced, properly speaking, as that of the jouissance of the Other. The correlative of the nightmare is the incubus or the succubus, a being who weighs with all of its opaque weight of alien jouissance on your chest, who crushes you under its jouissance. [...] The first thing that appears in the myth, but also in the experience of the nightmare, is that this being whose jouissance weighs on you is also a questioning being and even that it manifests itself in the fully developed dimension of the question that is called the enigma or riddle. (Lacan, 2004, p. 70)

The expression "the jouissance of the Other" is both a subjective and objective genitive, suggesting not only that we enjoy the Other, but also that the Other enjoys us, including all the questions raised by this opaque experience. The jouissance of the Other is therefore associated with the riddle of what the Other wants from us. This makes him an Other who is no longer complete—a lacking Other, or even an Other who has chosen us and loves us, as in the case of the vampire. The dimension of the Other's subjective lack, which borders on tragedy, is in fact a common element of modern vampire stories: either in the sense that the vampire's love for a human clashes with his nature—as we see in *Twilight*—or that the loss of a soulmate has made him melancholic—this is the case of Louis, the vampire narrator of Anne Rice's *Interview with the Vampire* (1976), who comes to tell his story to a human journalist.

On the other hand—and this is the most relevant to our discussion—Lacan, who was very interested in the question of frigidity, no longer makes the incubus the female partner of a nightmare, but rather a necessary condition of feminine jouissance, understood here in the most literal sense of the word. Lacan is rarely so explicit. As we are well aware, it is not enough for a straight woman to desire her lover in order to experience sexual pleasure; it is indeed a much more complicated operation. What, according to Lacan, is needed is a secret unconscious partner, hidden "behind the veil". This obscured man, whom the woman adores and who adores her in return, would then superimpose himself on to the real-life lover in order to make love to her. Unbeknown to her, the woman's jouissance arises from this phantasmatic embrace, which is transferred like a sheath on to her lover's penis—a transfer of jouissance worthy of the most fantastic imagination. But who is this obscured man, described by Lacan as "a castrated lover" or as a "dead man", in contrast to the real-life lover whose virility is in fact not at all contested? Lacan no doubt remembers the connection made by Jones between the incubus and incestuous desire. This site of adoration from which feminine jouissance originates would be the "ideal incubus", whom Lacan associates with the father in quite a unique way. This function of the father, as the "ideal incubus" has in fact received little attention in psychoanalytic literature. It is the father who stands beyond the mother and threatens the child with castration—currently referred to as the Name-of-the-father and his Law (Lacan, 2006b, p. 456)—but to the girl, as opposed to the boy, he poses "a threat of castration which does not really concern her". Because she knows she is a girl, she knows that there is nothing to castrate in her; but her jouissance derives from this empty threat, announced by the voice of a phantom—a transcendent and symbolic agency, Freud's dead father who becomes the Name-of-the-Father in Lacan. We now understand why this dead father, who has lost his castrating function and no longer has any use but to cause her jouissance in a secret embrace, is in fact the "ideal incubus".

Given the continuity between the incubus and the vampire, isn't the latter simply another, more popular name for the "ideal incubus", or the real partner of feminine jouissance? This could explain not only the constancy of the belief in vampires, which, as we have seen, is fuelled by feminine desire, but also its success in modern fiction. In addition, the vampire has many advantages over the incubus, as I shall now show by examining some of his literary appearances.

Literary vampires

The vampire myth proliferates in the nineteenth-century literature. *Dracula*, which was published in 1897 and inspired a number of plays and films, gained its notoriety thanks to its sophisticated postmodern composition—a combination of diary entries and letters. As a sickly child, its author Bram Stoker spent his time at home with his mother, the feminist writer Charlotte Matilda Thornley, who would often tell him legends and supernatural tales from Eastern Europe. Could he have been influenced by his mother's fantasies? The book's main narrator, Mina, is an intelligent woman and a writer, who is coveted by Dracula; her friend Lucy plays the essential role of the male vampire's erotic attractor. Lucy's human fiancé, though a fine man in all respects, cannot compete with the demonic attraction: Lucy becomes a vampire and must die a second death in order to save her soul.

Stoker was influenced by another Irish writer, Sheridan Le Fanu, the author of the wonderful novel *Carmilla* (1871), which was first made into a film by Dreyer (*Vampyr*, 1932) and again by Vadim (*To Die of Pleasure*, 1960). The narrator, Laura, tells the story of her seduction by Carmilla, a beautiful and sexy woman, a "vamp", as she would later aptly be called. Known under the different anagrams of her name, Millarca/Mircalla/Carmilla is the avatar of a Styrian countess, who had committed suicide because of a heartbreak. She spends her nights in a coffin or a bathtub filled with blood and falls in love with beautiful young girls who resemble her. In this novel of lesbian love, Carmilla tells Laura about the fascination that the young girl exerts on her, a fascination that goes far beyond the need for fresh blood:

> Think me not cruel because I obey the irresistible law of my strength and weakness; if your dear heart is wounded, my wild heart bleeds with yours. In the rapture of my enormous humiliation I live in your warm life, and you shall die—die, sweetly die—into mine. I cannot help it; as I draw near to you, you, in your turn, will draw near to others, *and learn the rapture of that cruelty, which yet is love.* (Sheridan Le Fanu, 2012, p. 36, my italics)

In a state between horror and ecstasy, Laura hears "one clear voice, of a female's, very deep", bringing her the experience of a certain transgressive jouissance, which returns as a leitmotif throughout the novel: "that pleasant, peculiar cold thrill which we feel in bathing, when we move against the current of a river" (Sheridan Le Fanu, 2012, p. 64).

Their love is both unique and predestined: as a child, each of them had a premonitory dream about the other (Sheridan Le Fanu, 2012, p. 10). *Carmilla* shows the split between love and the desire to kill, which haunts the vampire and provokes a subjective conflict that we find again in *Twilight*. At the same time, this duality exerts a powerful attraction on the chosen victim, even though the latter understands the criminal nature of her lover, and Carmilla's disappearance provokes an eternal, amorous nostalgia: "And to this hour the image of Carmilla returns to memory with ambiguous alternations—sometimes the playful, languid, beautiful girl; sometimes the writhing fiend I saw in the ruined church; and often from a reverie I have started, fancying I heard the light step of Carmilla at the drawing room door" (Sheridan Le Fanu, 2012, p. 124). The vampire thus represents a constitutive ambiguity, which cannot be reduced to his "non-dead" state: in order to be a lover like no other, the "ideal incubus" is neither man nor woman. Laura, too, wonders whether Carmilla is not actually a young man in disguise.

The vampire, who chooses his prey because of love, is a superb illustration of the "erotomaniacal form of love" (Lacan, 2006c, p. 617) that Lacan sees as characteristic of women. By throwing himself on his victim in the name of passion, the vampire effectively absolves her of any need to make amorous decisions, let alone take responsibility for her own desire. This forced consent, torn away from consciousness and experienced as a dream, touches upon the female fantasy of ravishment which we also see in other "non-vampiric" novels—for example in Kleist's *The Marquise of O*—and which finds evidence in clinical work. As I have mentioned, the Church focused on the degree to which the woman visited by the incubus consented to their union—and they were not without reason. Jones too makes the rejection of guilt for one's incestuous desire the reason why it is projected on to the incubus or vampire.

These vampiric characteristics appear in a number of other novels featuring a male predator who subjugates a young woman. For example, Pauline Réage's *The Story of O*, published in 1954, tells the story of O's unconditional love for René, who makes her his submissive, offering her to different men, who rape and beat her in a libertine institution. She accepts without batting an eyelid, as if it were some type of amorous mission, until one day René introduces her to Stephen, a kind of deeply admired older brother. Stephen is René's absolute master and, for the first time, O feels the pain of having been given over to someone completely. She feels betrayed by René because he values his relationship with Stephen more than her. Stephen makes O feel that she is an "easy" woman, suggesting that she in fact enjoyed complying with René's orders, instead of making a sacrifice for love as she had believed. A cruel and sadistic master, he makes O his sex slave, which includes putting her in chains and branding her with his cypher. From this moment on, the only thing that counts for O is to know whether Stephen is going to fall in love with her. Doesn't Stephen, as the locus of worship and of the ultimate and obscure sacrifice, take the position of the ideal incubus, of the master hiding behind O's lover René, with the latter eventually losing all importance for her, just like her own life? Even the most obscene sex scenes make the reader think of vampirism, which, after all, also invents new sexual orifices by making incisions in the body: the two small bites on the neck which are his "trademark". We see O's body reduced to solely its orifices, which, after having been pierced and artificially enlarged, are exposed to everyone's gaze and subject to the whims of Stephen and his guests. We also find an equivalent of the vampiric contamination, when O in turn acts as a sexual predator towards another young woman, whom she is supposed to serve up to her masters as a sex object.

A more recent novel by the American writer Joyce Carol Oates, *Beasts*,[21] which was published in 2002, and so preceding the *Twilight* saga, is also set on an American college campus. Gillian, an anorexic student of literature, has poetic aspirations and falls in love with her professor André, who is all students' object of worship. The love story begins with Gillian's erotomaniacal dream, in which she hears André's "low, confiding, consoling voice", proving to her that she is indeed the chosen one. André is married to a bizarre artist named Dorcas, who makes disturbing-looking sculptures of primitive female figures: one of them is carrying a man as if he were a child, smothered by the breast. The sculpture is a (slightly too) obvious metaphor for André's subjugation by his wife, who is portrayed as a kind of female ogre. Throwing herself into this obscure jouissance, Gillian first becomes André's lover and then the couple's sex toy; they drug her and take pictures of her in obscene poses. Gillian is in love with André, or perhaps with both of them—it is not entirely clear. However, what interests us is the way André is described: through a poem by D. H. Lawrence, which he offers to his students as a literary model to follow. "I love to suck you out from your skins" (Oates, 2003, p. 74), he recites to his ecstatic female audience; or: "Your triumph is in perfect submission. And the god of Eros will flow through you, as Lawrence says, in the 'perfect obliteration of blood consciousness'" (Oates, 2003, p. 61). In order to encourage her to become a good writer, André often tells Gillian, his *"morceau délicieux"* (Oates, 2003, p. 94), to "Go deeper. Go for the jugular!" (2003, p. 62).

Isn't this the behaviour of a vampire, who is both in love and thirsty for blood, and demands his victim's submission and self-sacrifice? Contrary to *Twilight*, in this case he does not hold back and consequently everything ends badly—with a sacrifice, just like in *The Story of O*, yet one that turns into murder. Another characteristic that Oates has managed to show very well is that, for the young girl, the Man or Vampire represents a "subject supposed to know how to enjoy". We find this trait in O's Stephen, in Christian Grey of Fifty Shades, and even in Edward from Twilight, whose jouissance is potentially lethal. Unlike *Fifty Shades*, the last two ambitious novels, *The Story of O* and *Beasts*, are not erotic romances—they are violent texts, where the predatory vampirism of the male character or vampire is explicitly sexual and is concealed neither by love nor by a subjective conflict that would make him more human. Also, the novels' graphic nature has by far prevented them from enjoying the same success among female readers.

At the same time, these more hardcore novels feature some of the traits that we also find in *Fifty Shades* and *Twilight*, albeit in a softer, repressed form:

- the figure of *Man* as an enigmatic or non-human being, a god or sexual master beyond all possible partners; a supernatural creature beyond gender, with a voice that subjugates;
- the apparently "chemical" attraction between the partners, which eliminates the woman's willpower;
- the suspension of her consent and responsibility for her own desire;
- the master's supposed knowledge about feminine jouissance;
- the violent invasion (breaking and entering) of the woman's body;
- the woman's fascination, temptation, submission and self-sacrifice;
- unconditional love; and
- initiation, and contamination by jouissance.

With the exception of bodily invasion, all these traits characterise the Lacanian complex of the "ideal incubus" as a version of the dead father. We could therefore argue that what we are dealing with here is a "complementary female complex" to the myth of the perverse father in *Totem and Taboo*, which Freud imagined solely with respect to the sons and their social and personal access to masculinity.

The vampire myth has the advantage of repressing genital sexuality into orality, thus making it compatible with censorship—this is why it primarily addresses young readers. At the same time, it foregrounds the violent opening of the female body which the fantasy of the ideal incubus concealed. However, fantastic fiction lets us accept more easily what we would reject in "normal" life—namely, behaviour that we find morally shocking or contrary to social and sexual ideals. Thanks to fantasy literature, we can live other lives, as if they were real, without anguish.

Finally, let us return to the two-fold reason for the global success of *Fifty Shades*. On the one hand, the plot celebrates a female hysteric who is able to subjugate the master through love, and to care for him, insofar as he is structurally castrated (Lacan, 2007, pp. 93–97). As a sex manual, the novel also encourages solitary pleasure, albeit one that is shared with other women in a community of a globalised hysterical trance. But, on the other hand, none of this would work without the underlying fantasy of the vampire, which touches upon the deepest layers of the feminine unconscious through the complex of the "ideal incubus".

The widespread success of *Fifty Shades* is nonetheless ironic. As Jones shows, historically the belief in vampires repressed the incestuous desire for the father, together with the excessively genital sexuality of the incubus. By imitating a vampire romance for teenagers, *Fifty Shades* has been able to ride the wave of *Twilight*'s success, whilst also explicitly reintroducing genital sexuality into its narrative. E. L. James has done so very skilfully, in a way that further softens the vampiric traits— deep down, *Fifty Shades* is much less shocking than, for example, *Breaking Dawn*. The liberating effect of this partial lifting of repression, which had weighed heavily on women for centuries, has no doubt been in part responsible for the massive popularity of a trilogy that otherwise boasts few literary qualities.

Notes

1. All my information comes from this excellent infographic website: http://neomam.com/fifty-shades-of-grey-infographic/.
2. Although the enormous sales figures are easily available, reliable information on the book's readership is harder to come by. Still, there is some data. In 2012, the US market research agency Bowker said that: "It's a remarkable phenomenon. Nearly one in five adult fiction books

purchased for women in June were from the Fifty Shades Trilogy", (Jo Henry, Director of Bowker Market Research, a service of ProQuest affiliate Bowker). And also: "Buyers of the Fifty Shades books are more likely to be women, live in the Northeast, and have a significantly higher household income. They read fewer paperbacks and more digital books versus last year and are especially likely to use a hand-held device such as a Kindle. Their purchase of a Fifty Shades book was more likely to be planned—just 11 per cent were whims—and oh yeah, nine out of ten times the purchase was for "pleasure/relaxation", but it's worth noting that an intriguing one per cent were purchased for "work/career" reasons." See "Who's Really Reading Fifty Shades?" available at: http://www.bowker.com/en-US/aboutus/press_room/2012/pr_11292012.shtml. The research done by the French institute IFOP and published in January 2013 shows that: "Reading erotica has become a widespread practice among women: nearly six out of ten (59%) admit that they have read an adult novel in their life, compared to slightly more than one in three in 1970 (38%). See: http://www.ifop.com/media/poll/2094-1-annexe_file.pdf.
3. BDSM stands for "bondage, discipline, domination and submission", where the mutual agreement between consenting adults is supposedly established on the model of the written contract in masochism.
4. The following paragraph refers to the author's interview "Ist Sadomasochismus die Lösung, Ein Gespräch mit Eva Illiouz", published in the *Frankfurter Allgemeine Zeitung* on 22 June 2013, p. 40 (my translation).
5. The origins of the English erotic romance date back to the eighteenth century; they were followed by a modernist revival before the First World War. The genre again became popular in 1930s England, with a number of specialised publishers, of which the most famous—Harlequin—was eventually established in Canada in the 1950s. The late 1980s saw the rise of a new subgenre of women's erotica featuring more graphic sexuality, contrary to the chaste stories that had been the key to Harlequin's success. The question is, why was none of these books as fortunate as *Fifty Shades*?
6. Parallel suggested by Sarah Grenier-Millette in *Écriture de l intime et littérature érotique au féminin*, available at: http://popenstock.ca/dossier/x-women, retrieved on 29 September 2013.
7. My italics. Here, the Other designates the locus of speech and language.
8. For example, the French journalist Gaëlle-Marie Zimmermann writes in a blog post for the *Nouvel Observateur* (22 October 2012): "It's nice and entertaining and although I have no intentions to go and buy a whip, I quite enjoyed fantasizing about it. This apparently means that

I have the literary tastes of a housewife. That could well be true—and I absolutely don't care." Or: "Fifty Shades simply turned me on and that was delightful. Am I ashamed to have completely devoured this idiotic novel? Absolutely not, regardless of the opinions of journalists, who look down on women aroused by this kind of prose."

See: http://leplus.nouvelobs.com/gaellemariezimmermann. Retrieved on 29 September 2013.

9. See her interview in Metronews, issue 18 October 2012, available online (French): http://www.metronews.fr/culture/e-l-james-cinquante-nuances-de-grey-n-est-pas-un-roman-pornographique/mljr!HkLrjUoSbp43g/.
10. This is also the story of another popular hero of our time, Don Draper from the US TV series *Mad Men*.
11. In other words, Lacan's object *a*: the fantasy links the subject divided by language to the object *a*, the cause of desire.
12. See *Mediabistro*: http://www.mediabistro.com/galleycat/fifty-shades-of-grey-wayback-machine_b49124. Retrieved on 29 September 2013.
13. Meyer quoted in *The Telegraph*, 11 March 2013: http://www.telegraph.co.uk/culture/twilight/9921818/Stephenie-Meyer-I-havent-read-Fifty-Shades-of-Grey.html. Retrieved on 29 September 2013.
14. See http://www.stepheniemeyer.com/bio.html and http://www.stepheniemeyer.com/twilight.html: "All this time, Bella and Edward were, quite literally, voices in my head. They simply wouldn't *shut up*. I'd stay up as late as I could stand trying to get all the stuff in my mind typed out, and then crawl, exhausted, into bed (my baby still wasn't sleeping through the night, yet) only to have another conversation start in my head."
15. I will cite only a few examples from the first volume of each series. There are of course many others.
16. Dom Calmet is the author of «Treaty on the Apparitions of Spirits and Vampires, or Ghosts of Hungary, Moravia, & c.» (1751).
17. An Abyssinian proverb quoted by Ernest Jones (1931, p. 183).
18. Jules Delassus, quoted in Jones (1931, p. 47). The female equivalent of the incubus is the succubus.
19. Lecouteux points out that starting from the sixteenth century the vampire basically replaces the incubus or the nightmare in attacking the sleeper (2009, p. 75).
20. He goes on to add: "The main differences are that hate and guilt play a far larger part in the Vampire than in the Incubus belief, where the emotions are purely those of desire and fear" (Jones, 1931, p. 130).
21. Translator's note: the French title of the novel, *Délicieuses pourritures*, refers to the "delicious rottenness" of Lawrence's poem cited in the book.

References

Freud, S. (1921). Group Psychology and the Analysis of the Ego. *S. E., 18*: 67. London: Hogarth.
Gilbert, J. A. (2009). Le modèle du sang: une économie de la damnation. In: N. Noyaret (Ed.), *Le Vampirisme et ses Formes dans Les Lettres et les Arts* (pp. 47–63). Paris: L'Harmattan.
Illouz, E. (2012). *Why Love Hurts: A Sociological Explanation*. Cambridge: Polity Press.
James, E. L. (2011). *Fifty Shades of Grey*. London: Vintage Books, 2012.
Jones, E. (1931). *On the Nightmare*. London: Hogarth.
Lacan, J. (2001). Introduction à l'édition allemande d'un premier volume des Écrits. In: *Autres écrits*. Paris: Seuil.
Lacan, J. (2004). *Le Séminaire Livre X, L'angoisse*. Paris: Seuil.
Lacan, J. (2006a). Position of the unconscious. In: *Écrits: The First Complete Edition in English* (Transl. B. Fink) (pp. 703–721). New York: Norton.
Lacan, J. (2006b). On a question prior to any possible treatment of psychosis In: *Écrits: The First Complete Edition in English* (Transl. B. Fink) (pp. 445–488). New York: Norton.
Lacan, J. (2006c). Guiding remarks for a convention on female sexuality. In: *Écrits: The First Complete Edition in English* (Transl. B. Fink) (pp. 610–622). New York: Norton.
Lacan, J. (2007). *The Seminar, Book XVII, The Other Side of Psychoanalysis*. New York: Norton.
Lecouteux, C. (2009). *Histoire des Vampires*. Paris: Imago.
Meyer, S. (2005). *Twilight*. New York: Little, Brown, 2006.
Meyer, S. (2010). *Breaking Dawn*. London: Atom.
Oates, J. C. (2003). *Beasts*. London: Orion.
Rice, A. (1976). *Interview with the Vampire*. New York: Random House.
Sheridan Le Fanu, J. T. (2012). *Carmilla*. Toronto: The House of Pomegranates Press.

CHAPTER SIX

Hysteria, a hystory

Colette Soler

Translated by Kristina Valendinova

Speaking about hysterics, Lacan used the word "hystorics". The equivocation was intriguing, but it could easily pass for just a clever throwaway line. I would like to consider its implications. Its meaning is twofold: first, that hysterics tell stories,[1] and we must ask about those stories, and how they are being told. Yet it also means that, historically, hysteria has always been in a state of flux: it changes, at least in form, so we can say that, depending on the context, the stories hysterics tell us are not always the same.

I should remind you that when we say "hysteria", which, in French, is a feminine noun, it tells us nothing about the hysterics' sex—they may be male or female. Neither can hysteria be defined solely on the basis of one type of symptom; the so-called mechanism of conversion, from psyche into soma, as they used to say. In Freud's time, these conversion phenomena represented a great intellectual challenge because they showed the degree to which language and discourse can have an effect on what, precisely, is not language—namely the organism. The problem is that conversion is not hysteria's prerogative. This "speaking with one's body" (as Lacan puts it in *Encore*: "I speak with my body and

I do so unbeknownst to myself. Thus I always say more than I know", 1998, p. 119), discovered by psychoanalysis in its very beginnings, is not specific to hysteria. It is a formula of what I have called a "generalised conversion"—only this "speaking with one's own body" speaks all by itself. We know that the symptom, whatever form it takes, is always self-sufficient, and that we need the artifice of discourse in order for it to become a demand, a form of address. In other words, we need to insert the symptom into a social bond. The drive itself asks for nothing. True, it is searching for something—the surplus enjoyment in the place of the Other—but it takes it without asking permission. The drive always authorises itself.

Hystory with a y

It was in the 1970 Seminar XVII, *The Other Side of Psychoanalysis* (Lacan, 2007), as well as in *Radiophonie*, recorded in the same year, that Lacan designated hysterical structure as a specific type of social bond. Likewise in the 1976 seminar *L'insu que sait* ["The Unknown that Knows"],[2] hysterics were again renamed "hystorics", while around the same time Lacan also began writing hystory with a y. The argument is complicated and it could not have been formulated at an earlier time.

I will begin with hystory. Is this to say that the historical course of events is hysterical? Not necessarily, but it does mean that events only become a history once they have been told. The French expression "*raconter des histoires*" has a double meaning: it refers to lying, but also, and more interestingly, to the formation of the signifying chain. To put this another way, hystory only exists through the signifying chain, through *storytelling*,[3] as they say today. Sartre might have said it exists through the novel. It only exists in the stories we tell/make up, and these stories not only constitute a social bond, but also they can only be narrated in the context of such a bond. We are always telling a story to someone or for someone, whether it is for posterity, as Jean-Jacques Rousseau would say, or for future centuries of scholars, as alluded to by James Joyce. To Plato, who tells us the story of Socrates, we should therefore add Hegel—in Lacan's view "the most sublime hysteric" (2007, p. 35)—who invented the phenomenological epic of the master and slave, dreaming about absolute knowledge at the end of hystory. What an illusion! This helps us understand to what extent all hystories, even the best ones, always lie, since they are trying to do the impossible: to convert the

Real into a signifier. Also, think of the present-day competition between different hystorical memories.

As for calling hysteria historical, this means that it is constantly shifting, depending on the movement of social history, specifically depending on the changes that affect the S1, the master signifier, the hysteric's partner. It is then up to us to examine today's situation in terms of both the S1 and the hysterical subjects related to it. This is a very difficult question, and all the work is still to be done because so far we don't seem to have shed any light on it.

Lacan shows that this was equally true for prior historical periods: here too we can identify not just one type of hysteria but an entire range. Therefore we should really be speaking about hysterias, while specifying which elements can and cannot change. The structure of the hysterical social bond does not change—it is transhistorical. Judging from the writing of its discourse, we can therefore already say that the strategy remains the same for both Socrates and Dora, the two emblematic figures of hysteria, which explains why Lacan also called the hysterias "Socratic". What nonetheless does differ is the master, the S1, to which they are both speaking, and therefore also the product, that is, the knowledge the discourse creates. Hence we must distinguish between what I have called "the Freudian hysterias" and the hysteria of Socrates. Both are based on a double condition. The Freudian hysterias are determined by two factors: on the one hand, contemporary discourse; on the other hand, the Freudian operation. These were basically the hysterics of the nineteenth century: women who remained confined, by the morality of their time, to the realm of the marital couple and the family—just like Flaubert's *Madame Bovary*. I have called them Freudian hysterics because it was their encounter with the Freudian method that allowed them to tell Freud the history of the Oedipus complex and introduce the question of sexuality into scientific discourse, from which it had previously been—like the question of the subject—excluded. I will come back to this. For these hysterics who came to psychoanalysis, the S1 they questioned was therefore embodied by a Man with a capital M, one who was supported by the master-signifier of sex, the phallus (in all senses of the word "support").[4] In the Freudian framework, who could respond to this question? Clearly not the man himself: as Lacan says, the answer could only be produced by "letting the Other speak", meaning the Other with a capital O, the site of the signifier; in other words, by letting the signifying structure of the unconscious speak, which produces the symptom. In the course of an analysis, hysteria therefore produced the answer that language gives about sex. Freud and Lacan formulated this answer as "there is no sexual relationship"; there is only the One [*Y a d'l'Un*] and nothing else. That was of course not the answer hysterics had been waiting for.

Socrates' role is entirely different: his partner is not the S1 of sexuality but the S1 of politics. He is speaking to the lords of the city; he does not question knowledge about sexuality. True, in the story told by Alcibiades he refuses to offer his body to the master's jouissance;[5] however, there is no doubt that his aim, while being perfectly hysterical, is nevertheless not the same as in the case of the Freudian hysterics. Undoubtedly thanks to Plato, Socrates is therefore at the origin of what Lacan calls the longest transference in history. By calling on the master's lack, he manages to create a desire for knowledge. But what kind of knowledge is this? Certainly not knowledge about sex, as Lacan explains in *Radiophonie*:

> The hysteric [...] puts the master up against the wall to produce knowledge. [...] Such was the ambition induced in the Greek master under the name of episteme. [...] [by which] he was summoned, and namely by a hysterical Socrates [...] to show something that justified his powers as a master. (2001, p. 436)

A little later, Lacan says that the result of this was science. There is no question of sex here. The Freudian hysterics therefore represent the return of whatever the Socratic hysteria historically failed to produce. We can then understand Lacan when he says that the discourse of science has virtually the same structure as the discourse of hysteria because science indeed puts the One to work in order to produce knowledge. This would be a good reason to speak about "scientific hysteria", but the One of this kind of hysteria, if you will, would no longer be the One of Socratic hysteria, and neither yet the One of the Freudian kind, as if the structure of hysteria could produce very diverse effects—as diverse as the S1, its partner master-signifier.

The storyette of the hys-trique[6]

This brings us to the stories of hysteria. That hysterics are indeed hystorics who tell or make up stories is obvious: simply because it is the unconscious—which, thanks to them, Freud was able to discover—that is in fact telling these stories or, if you will, the unconscious signifying chain, which in any case is the same thing. This is one way of putting it, and it will perhaps help you understand the difference I have tried to make between the unconscious as language [*l'inconscient langage*] and the real unconscious [*l inconscient réel*] (Soler, 2014, p. 33). The latter does not tell any stories. Instead, it provokes the emergence of parasitic elements in speech, behaviour, and scope of attention, from slips of the tongue to symptoms and including bungled actions and dreams. The Freudian operation of decoding, which does not originate from the unconscious, turns it into a signifying chain, into the history of the signified, so very difficult to grasp and determine—the so-called unconscious desire. But what is the Freudian hysteric's favourite story? She speaks about the father and accordingly about the mother—she complains about her, denounces her as the source of various frustrations, which all fall under the heading of *Penisneid*. And how is she telling her story? With her mouth, no doubt, through her words, but also through her symptoms, which speak once they have been deciphered. That was what gave Freud an inkling of the Oedipus complex, which binds the generations together. In his lecture on Joyce, Lacan calls this complex a "storyette" [*historiole*]—and he means it pejoratively. It is on this issue that he takes the firmest stance against Freud, in his 1969–1970 seminar The Other Side of Psychoanalysis (2007). Nevertheless, in the same lesson of the seminar, and still speaking about the discourse of the hysteric, he also begins to introduce the topic of the hysteric's father. This contradiction raises the question of what function we should ultimately attribute to the hysteric's story.

To answer, I have to make a bit of a leap. More than ten years later, in his seminar *L'insu que sait (1976–77)* (1977–78), Lacan argued that the hysteric "only has an unconscious to make her consistent, it is radically other. She even is not, except as Other".[7] The entire seminar, but especially these first two lessons, are very difficult. Nevertheless, I believe we can still grasp a certain number of elements.

My first remark is this: in the ALI transcription that I am using (Lacan, 1976–1977), the Other is written with a small "o", but I think we should capitalise it because, later in the same seminar, Lacan says that one cannot recognise oneself in the unconscious, that it remains Other, radically Other with a capital O. Hysteria is radically Other, just like the unconscious, and therefore it is impossible to reason with. Having made this argument about hysteria, he adds: "And that is my own case, me too, I only have the unconscious. That is the reason I think about it all the time" and says that he is a perfect hysteric—a symptomless one. I will leave aside what concerns only Lacan himself and instead pay attention to what he says about the hysteric in general. Like the analyst, the hysteric only has the unconscious in order to produce consistency— we must therefore assume that others owe their consistency to something else.

In this passage, "consistency" means that a body receives signifiers, which give it substance [*reçoit du corps des signifiants*]. Lacan even says that the material (i.e., the analysand's utterances) "is presented to us as corps-sistance,[8] in other words the subsistence of the body, i.e. what is consistent, what holds together."[9] However, the material is bipolar, meaning that S1 always refers to S2 and these two poles are corps-sistent. The corps-sistent material therefore includes not only the symptom's function of jouissance (corresponding to S2) but also the signifiers of identification (S1), to which Lacan devoted the preceding lesson of his seminar, where he reminded his students of the three forms of identification distinguished by Freud. To these three types of identification he tried to assign three ways of turning the torus, in order to bring the inside out, which transforms it into a rod [*trique*]. Instead of hys-torical consistency we should therefore speak of a hys-triqual one.

Lacan adds that the hysteric is sustained in her "rod" structure "by a framework [*armature*], which is distinct from her consciousness [...] It is her love for her father." The Freudian Oedipus complex is therefore contrasted with the hysteric's love for the father. The S1 of the father constitutes her framework, yet one she has no knowledge of and which is removed from her consciousness. In *The Other Side of Psychoanalysis* Lacan pointed out that the knowledge produced by her discourse remains alien to the hysteric, so that ultimately we could say that it is not really her knowledge. Here he adds that her love for the father, and the identification associated with it, are too removed from consciousness. This is a bit strange. Let us look at what happens clinically. What presence does the father have in the hysteric's consciousness? Her feelings for him seem to be the very opposite of love. Isn't it true that the discourse about the father we normally hear from the hysteric, in the form of a complaint, is utterly debasing? He is portrayed as deficient, as lacking in terms of desire or the phallic function. Unless, of course, the subject instead denounces the father of jouissance, which is less common. This conscious discourse, which in either case stigmatises the father's degraded image as lacking in desire, is not really a discourse of love. What manages to reach consciousness is a kind of trial, a judgment of the father's inadequacies, often in the form of a reproach, either for not having kept the mother in check, or for having neglected her. The same attitude is then generally adopted towards the father of the hysteric's children, if such a person exists.

The Other Side of Psychoanalysis explains this very simply. The father, who is criticised for being "out of action" (2007, p. 95)—an expression Lacan uses about Dora's father—this impotent father, whom I have described as degraded, is what he calls the ideal father. He says this more than once. Speaking about the castrated master or father: "This is the proper function, identified a long time ago, at least in my school, under the title of the idealized father" (p. 107). How should we understand this? Quite simply that we can only denounce a reality, in this case the reality of a father, based on some idea; in order to criticise her father, the hysteric necessarily maintains a normative idea of what a father should be. This is expressed as: "The word 'father' designates someone who can still potentially create", even if in reality he is faulty or insufficient. The creation in question is what figures in his relationship to the woman: the creation of the progenitor, of procreation. However insufficient he may have become, he can never fall from his function with respect to the woman; like an ex-soldier, he will always remain an ex-progenitor. The dearly loved father remains in the unconscious as the reverse side of the hysteric's conscious diatribe against him, and this represents the hysteric's insertion in the generational order. This is then, according to Lacan, the Freudian hysteric's favourite hy/story, and the remainder of her Oedipal romance. Freud was the one to collect its elements, yet Lacan is able to turn it into a lesson on jouissance, which itself does not tell any stories but becomes manifest in action, in the subject's conduct.

The asexual symptoms of the hys-trique

Clinically speaking, the key phenomenon of hysteria is what I would call a systematic lack of satisfaction, that is, a lack that is cultivated, to distinguish it from the generic dissatisfaction of any speaking being. This has given rise to a series of different interpretations: first it was the manifestation of a desire to desire, then it was necessary to keep jouissance unsatisfied so that desire can be sustained. But any desire is always linked to a modality of jouissance. As for the desire to desire, you surely know how it has been reformulated, reinterpreted in terms of jouissance: "the jouissance of being deprived" (2007, p. 99), "the body on strike" (p. 94), and "identification with the jouissance of the castrated master" (p. 97). All these come from *The Other Side of Psychoanalysis*, which will help us clarify the jouissance in question. When Lacan says about the hysteric that she does not want jouissance, he uses the case of Dora as a clinical illustration. By telling Dora: "My wife means nothing to me", Herr K is offering her his jouissance, but she does not want it—just as Socrates refuses young Alcibiades' advances. However, the thing she does not want is what Lacan beautifully calls "the good old orgasm" [*le bon gros jouir*], namely the jouissance of the organ, or the one that comes via the organ in relationships we improperly call sexual. Like Socrates in his response to Agathon, Dora leaves that kind of jouissance to someone else, to Frau K, who, as Lacan argues, knows how to contain what corresponds to this desire and thus simultaneously deprive Dora of it.

The chapter on the discourse of the hysteric is built on a sharp distinction between the jouissance of the phallic organ in sexual intercourse and that of surplus-enjoyment as a condition of the master's knowledge. The master is castrated but surplus-enjoyment is returned to him. Lacan says: "By simply fulfilling his function as master, he loses something. (…) And through this loss at least something is restored to him—precisely surplus-enjoyment" (p. 107), which, by the way, in the formula of the [master's] discourse stands in the position of production, where knowledge determines surplus-enjoyment.

Therefore, the master is not deprived of surplus-enjoyment—quite the opposite, he dominates it—but he can only accumulate surplus-enjoyment on the condition of excluding phallic jouissance. Lacan even speaks of the master's "rage to castrate himself and to take into account the surplus-enjoyment [...] on which capitalism was founded" (ibid.). And, before capitalism, science. Hence we can conclude that the aforementioned "strike" of the body is far from being a total one because surplus-enjoyment is always retained. Lacan illustrates this using the example of bedwetting, a common symptom. It is a stigma, he says, of the child's imaginary identification with the father as, precisely, impotent. Yet we should also remember the connection between bedwetting and ambition. As a derivation of phallic jouissance outside the sphere of sex, ambition skilfully diverts us from the latter's dead ends. Now, we know that hysterical subjects are not exactly exempted from this. And this should in fact help us to understand hysteria today, as our age has certainly not marked the end of the castrated master's jouissance. It was due to their identification with this jouissance that Freud's hysterics would go through the entire range of possibilities offered by the drive, through the different forms of surplus-enjoyment—oral, anal, etc. Here again, Dora has left her mark. Just think of the symptomatic cough, her identification with the impotent father's enjoyment, which finds a suppletion in the oral fantasy of fellatio or cunnilingus: impotence doesn't deprive one of the oral means required by these kinds of jouissance. All of this concerns a form of hysteria that I would describe as specialising in asexual jouissance. It remains then to examine its sexual symptom. To say that the body is "on strike" is not incorrect, but after all it does not tell us very much. Plus, Lacan did in fact return to this question, trying to explain what the properly sexual symptom of hysteria was—one that cannot be reduced either to a strike or to asexual surplus-enjoyment.

The sexual symptom of the hysteric

In the second chapter of *Joyce avec Lacan* Lacan discusses the hysterical symptom in relation to his notion of "woman as a symptom" introduced in Seminar XXII R.S.I. in 1975. Here in *Joyce le symptôme II*, he returns to his previous argument by saying that "the individuals which Aristotle considers to be bodies can themselves be nothing but symptoms for other bodies. For example, a woman can be just a symptom of another body. If that is not the case, she remains a so-called hysterical symptom" (Lacan, 1987, p. 35). Here we have a definition of the couple: a body and its symptom, who is another body. We have come to the notion of what Lacan calls the last symptom (I sometimes say the fundamental symptom), one which, despite the fact that the "one" jouissance does not create a relationship, nonetheless manages to invisibly hold together at least two bodies, where any relationship between their jouissances is lacking. This symptom is non-autistic and does not call for therapy: it acts as a solution to the absence of a rapport.

Now, the hysteric is not a symptom of another body. She is defined by the fact that, I quote, "the only thing that interests [her] is another symptom. [...] To sum up, the hysterical symptom is the symptom of a LOM [*l'homme*] being interested in another's symptom as such—[an interest] which does not require bodily contact" (ibid.). Neither has it anything to do with hysterical conversion. And here we must go back to Socrates as hysteria's perfect model. Not the Socrates whose desire and maieutics question the political master, but Socrates as a sexed individual within the Greek homosexual community. Which is enough to say that the sexual symptom of hysteria does not imply heterosexuality. Remember that Alcibiades's story of his youthful adventures with Socrates highlights the latter's strategy of phallic deprivation.[10] Here, Lacan tries to formulate a definition of jouissance which he takes directly from sex. Having listened to Alcibiades' account, Socrates replies that the entire story was addressed to someone else present, namely to Agathon, Socrates's current partner, and, we could say, his current partner-symptom. Lacan then formulates his interpretation of the sexual symptom of hysteria: Socrates, the perfect hysteric, "was fascinated by the symptom alone—snatched from the other" (ibid). Fascination is the important word—you will recall that Lacan uses the same expression for Dora's relationship to Frau K and to the Madonna.

This means that there are always three elements involved in the hysterical symptom: the hysteric, the other, and the other's symptom. And what we see here is another way of invisibly holding bodies together—it is not a sexual relationship but a fine "social knot", binding together at least three individuals. Hysteria has the unique ability to create a social bond using precisely what it excludes: the sexual jouissance of two bodies in a sexed couple. We should take note of Lacan's very precise formulation—hysteria is interested in the other's symptom and interests the other's symptom—also because it brings us to a slightly different reading of Dora's interest in Frau K. She is interested in her insofar as she supposes her to be a man's symptom. A symptom is more than a cause of desire; it is more than the slightly skinny friend of the beautiful butcher's wife. Socrates takes things further: he is interested in Alcibiades' symptom in the sense that he makes it obvious to everyone and thus prefigures the analyst and his interpretation. What Lacan is talking about here is therefore no longer an identification with the jouissance of the other, as in the case of deprival and surplus-jouissance. Rather the hyphenated inter-est implies the idea of being *inter* symptoms: the "second-to-last" symptom of hysteria, as Lacan calls it, essentially forges a bond with another symptom. Hysteria therefore represents a perfect symptom-bond [*symptôme lien*], which may exist in both a hetero- and homosexual version. This also means that the so-called homosexuality of the female hysteric is not at all the same homosexuality as that of the lesbian, because in the second case the bodily encounter is not lacking. In the sexual symptom, properly speaking, which invisibly holds two bodies together in spite of the absence of the sexual relationship, one body becomes an event for another, yet this does not create a social bond. That is the paradox, but also the triumph of hysteria; it is able to turn its symptom into a social bond, whereas the symptom as jouissance, as what is most real in each of us, is excluded from the established social bond. Hysteria is a symptom-bond, if I may put it this way, and that is why it permanently reminds us not of the truth of castration, as in the case of the fetish in perversion (see the last page of the *Écrits*), but of the real in the symptom. Lacan thus moves from hysteria's inter-subjectivity, which he emphasised in the beginning, to what I would call its inter-symptomatology.

In addition, Socrates' case shows us that the hysterical symptom is not principally heterosexual: as Lacan says, "everyman [*toutom, tout homme*] has a right to it". A right—isn't that surprising? Usually when we speak of having a right to something, this thing must be valuable. And Lacan continues: it is not simply a question of right but "a superiority, made obvious by Socrates". I have explained, I believe it was in *What Lacan Said about Women* (Soler, 2005), that this superiority has to do with the fact that male hysteria in some sense confronts us with hysteria in its pure state. This is because, for women, the question of femininity somewhat obscures the properly hysterical interest in the other's symptom. You see how far we have travelled: the hysterical question is no longer "What is a woman?" as Lacan initially said about the female hysteric as the symptom of psychoanalysis. Its more fundamental question, which Socrates exemplifies better than Dora, is "What is the other body's symptom?" And here the other is not capitalised because it is an individualised other. "What is a woman?" then becomes simply one version of a more general interrogation.

This symptom-bond is obviously all the more valuable at a time when social relations are becoming increasingly fragile, and it is always relative to their current forms. I have already mentioned the position of women at the time of the Freudian hysteric. The hysteria of Socrates, on the other hand, appears against the backdrop of quite a different social symptom, by which I mean the historically determined manner in which the political and social Other, here indeed spelled with a capital O, treats and manages human bodies. Socrates belongs "to a time when the common LOM [*l'homme*] had not yet been reduced to cannon fodder, although he had already been caught up in the deportation of bodies." This has absolutely nothing to do with the question of women. Deportations were common practice in Ancient Greece, on a more limited scale than in modern times, but Plato himself was deported and spent some time in slavery. Still we might be surprised at Lacan's use of the "cannon fodder"[11] metaphor in a reference to our own day and age. This was in 1976—the image might seem slightly outdated with respect to the most recent war, and perhaps more in line with the First World War. Yet we call it the First War, although there had been so many before it, precisely because it was the first mechanised war, a "storm of steel" as the German officer Ernst Jünger has put it in his eponymous memoir. When responding to the second question in *Radiophonie*, at the very end, Lacan uses another image which chimes with "cannon fodder": he speaks about "the party fodder, used as the babysitter of history" to describe the unprecedented phenomenon of the great mobilisations of the masses by the two main parties of the twentieth century: the Communist and the Nazi Party, in spite of their many differences. The idea of "cannon fodder" is then not as outdated as we might think and refers to the mass exterminations facilitated by the great advances in weaponry; these indeed began during the 1914 war, but subsequent wars have only increased them.

In any case we should note that when Lacan is speaking about the symptom's singular way of treating the body, which is what the hysteric is interested in, he cannot but place it in the larger context of its collective treatment. This is where hysteria's sexual symptom, whether we are speaking of the Socratic or Freudian variety, takes on its value of constantly aiming at symptomatic singularity, whereas the social symptom only produces sameness, an all-of-us-ness—in today's version an "all-of-us-proletarians-ness". In other words, it lacks any means to create a social bond.

Notes

1. Translator's note: As the author herself points out later on, the double meaning of the French *raconter des histoires*—not only to "tell stories" but "to make things up, to lie"—is obviously crucial here.

2. Lacan, 1976–1977. The author is quoting from the version established by the Association lacanienne internationale (ALI) and available from its library in Paris (http://www.freud-lacan.com).
3. Translator's note: In English in the original: rather than to narration or narrative in general, in today's French, *storytelling* usually refers to particular kinds of discursive strategies used (or abused) for the purposes of marketing or propaganda.
4. Translator's note: *supporter* means to support, keep up, but also to tolerate, accept.
5. In the very last section of the *Symposium*.
6. Translator's note: Lacan's pun emphasises the rod-like [*trique*] structure of the hysteric, see below.
7. Seminar of 14 December 1976.
8. Translator's note: a play on *corps* (body) and *consistence* (consistency).
9. See p. 20 of the ALI transcription (Lacan, 1976–1977).
10. At the end of *The Symposium*, after the official speeches have been made.
11. Translator's note: In *chair à canon*, the French equivalent of "cannon fodder", *chair* literally means "flesh" or "meat". This is later paraphrased by Lacan's *chair à parti*, "party fodder" or meat, see below.

References

Lacan, J. (1976–77). *Séminaire Livre XXIV, Linsu que sait de l'une-bévue s'aile à mourre*. Transcription established by the Association Lacanienne Internationale. Unpublished.
Lacan, J. (1977–78). *L insu que sait de l'une-bévue s'aile à mourre* (Séminaire 1976–1977). *Ornicar?*, 12/13 (1977), 14/15 (1978).
Lacan, J. (1987). Joyce le symptôme II (1975). In: J. Aubert (Ed.), *Joyce avec Lacan*. Paris: Navarin.
Lacan, J. (1998). *The Seminar, Book XX, Encore. The Limits of Love and Knowledge* (Trans. B. Fink). New York: Norton.
Lacan, J. (2001). Radiophonie. *Autres écrits*. Paris: Seuil.
Lacan, J. (2007). *The Seminar, Book XVII, The Other Side of Psychoanalysis* (Trans. R. Grigg). New York: Norton.
Soler, C. (2005). *What Lacan Said About Women*. New York: Other Press.
Soler, C. (2014). *Lacan—The Unconscious Reinvented* (Trans. S. Schwartz & E. Faye). London: Karnac.

CHAPTER SEVEN

... As if I did not know ... (Allurement)

Vincent Dachy

One day you are flicking through a magazine of some entertaining nature with the appropriate absentminded attitude when, inadvertently, you bump into a questionnaire. Usually you do not give it half a glance. But this time is different, the title reads "What kind of woman are you?" Irresistible.

Here it is.

Discover, at last, your "proton aletheia"

Please answer "Yes" or "No" to all questions below.

1. Sometimes I really do not know who I am.
2. Is, sometimes, nostalgia an exquisite pain?
3. Do you think Proust was right?
4. Do you accept necessity?
5. Does not knowing it trouble you exquisitely?
6. Do you like St Augustine?
7. The true truth is a matter of feeling?
8. Sometimes saying "no" is the only way to really feel "yes"?
9. Vulnerable people are the proof of the existence of God?

10. Do you feel special in the neighbourhood of a boundary?
11. In society, do you speak first or second?
12. The snake of the Garden of Eden was cute.
13. Shouting can be the best way to keep silent.
14. Was Antigone's death worthwhile?
15. Do you know of a word that gives you an itch?
16. Do you believe in the structure?
17. Do you accept necessity now that you have answered these questions?

Answers overleaf

If you have wanted to answer "may be" and "'perhaps" to most questions,

You are reasonable and all is good if you believe it.

If you have wanted to throw away the magazine a few times during the reading of the questionnaire,

You cheeky thing but subversion may still lie a little way away.

If you have answered "yes" to all questions above,

You are right but it might have been a fluke.

If you have answered "no" to all questions above,

You are even more correct or were you just moody?

If you don't remember most of your answers,

You are eligible for the next issue of "What kind of woman are you?"

If you'd have wished someone had called while you were wondering about all the above,

Try to focus next time, daydreaming does not protect from everything.

Now try to answer the questionnaire again and truly know what kind of woman you really are.

INDEX

Abbott, M. 41
"abstinence porn" 68
Adair, M. J. 3
Affect of the Real, The 23
Akagi, H. 49
ALI transcription 89
American Psychiatric
　　　Association 46
"amorous illusions" 72
analytic derivations 54
anxiety 12, 17–18
　　hysteria 11–15
　　phobia and 14
　　pure states of 18
　　state of 14
　　treatment of 14–15
Appignanesi, L. 35
Assoun, P. -L. 17
astasia abasia 9
Austin, J. L. 44

BDSM 81
Beasts 64, 78–79
Bodies That Matter 44
Bollas, C. 35, 38, 40
Borossa, J. 40–41, 49
bourgeois family 43
Breaking Dawn 68, 80
British Psychoanalytic Council
　　46
Butler, J. 44–47

"cannon fodder" 96
Carmilla 76
castration 13, 22
"cause of desire" 67
Civilization and its Discontents 6
"consistency" 90
"constructive solutions" 59
"contemporary hysteria" 59
conversion hysteria 3–4, 12, 15–16

Corfield, D. 15
cultural value, of hysteria 21–23

Da Vinci Code, The 63
Daphnis and Chloe romance 65
Day of Judgment 71
De Lauretis, T. 42, 47–48
Deary, L. J. 35
deportations 96
depression 18–19
dérobade 29
Diagnostic and Statistical Manual of Mental Disorders 1
"decadent era" 65
"diabolic possession" 53
Dracula 75–76

Ego and The Id, The 45
"erotic romance stories" 64
"erotomania" 72
"erotomaniacal form of love" 77

Federn, E. 19, 29
Fifty Shades 63–70, 79–80
Fifty Shades Darker 63
Fifty Shades Freed 63
Fifty Shades of Grey 63
Foucault, M. 43
founding myths 42–43
Freud, S. 1–2, 4–12, 14–15, 17, 19, 27, 30–31, 41, 45, 47–49, 65

gender identity 45–46
Gender Trouble 44–45
Gherovici, P. 37
globus hystericus 35, 48
Grosz, E. 41–42
Guir, J. 16

Harris, M. B. 35
"Harry Potter" series 63
Hennessy, R. 41–42

History of Sexuality, The 43
holophrase 16
homosexuality 36–37, 41–49
House, A. 49
hysteria 88–89
    after Freud 4–11
    and perversion 19–21
    and psychosomatic phenomena 15–19
    anxiety 11–15
    asexual symptoms 91–93
    conversion 3–4, 12, 15–16
    cultural value of 21–23
    diagnostic confusion 28–33
    etymology of 3
    history of 1–4
    psychoanalysis and 35–41
    psychoanalytic vocabulary 8–9
    sexual symptom 93
    symptom 93
    symptoms and signs 2
    "hysterical-religious", hallucinations 72
hysteric's discourse 22
hysteric-to-be 37
"hystorics" 85

ideal incubus 74–75, 77, 79
Illouz, E. 64
"impurity" 61
inherent bisexuality 40, 49
Inhibitions, Symptoms and Anxiety 18
Interview with the Vampire 74

James, E. L. 66, 69
Jones, E. 72–73
Joyce le symptôme II 93

Lacan, J. 2, 7, 9, 13–14, 16–17, 21–23, 31–32, 37, 39, 65, 74–75, 77, 80, 86, 89, 93, 97
    "jouissance" 69

Laplanche, J. 35
Leader, D. 15
Lecouteux, C. 71
L'insu que sait 86, 89
literary vampires 75

Mad Men and Medusas 38
Marquise of O, The 77
Master of the Universe 68
mechanism of conversion 85
Merck, M. 47
Meyer, S. 68–69
Mitchell, J. 38–40
Moncayo, R. 35
"metaphor" 55
"metonymy" 55
"modern medicine" 53
"mommy porn" 63
"morceau délicieux" 79
myth of the vampire 71

necessity and seduction
    analytic derivations 54
    arrangement 56–57
    necessity versus contingency 58
    onset 53
    realm of love, nevertheless 57–58
    seduction 55–56
    shock 55
    symptom and simulation 54
    transfer and expression 54–55
Niederschriften 9
Nouvel Observateur 81
Nunberg H. 19, 29

Oates, J. C. 78–79
Oedipal conflict 39, 45
On the Nightmare 71
Other body 31–33
Other Minds 28–29

Other Side of Psychoanalysis The 86, 89–92, 95
Other Woman 30–31

Penisneid 89
personal identity 11
perversion 19–21
"perversion" 61
phobia 14
"piece of truth" 54
Pisk, G. 27
Plato 3
Pontalis, J. -B. 35
psychoanalytic discourse 7–8
psychosis 28–30, 32
psychosomatic phenomena 15–19

qua 18
queer
    definition of 42
    new site of hysteria 48–49
    psychoanalysis and 41–46
    resonances with hysteria and 46–48
Queer theory 41–48

"raconteur des histoires" 86
Radiophonie 86
"repression" 55
Rice, A. 74
"rod" structure 90
revendication 39
Rodríguez, L. 14–15, 17
Rosenfeld, H. 32
Ryan, J. 47

Sachs, H. 19, 21
Safouan, M. 28
Salih, S. 41
"scientific hysteria" 88
Sedgwick, E. 47
Sepel, Colette 23

sex and gender 43–46
sexual identity 33, 45
Sheridan Le Fanu, J. T. 76–77
Sinfield, A. 41
"social knot" 94
sociological approach The 64
Soler, C. 17, 89, 95
somatic compliance 15
Story of O, The 64, 77, 79
Studies on Hysteria 31
"subjective arrangement" 61
Sullivan, 2003 41
supple chain 32
symptom-bond 95

"tasty" anecdotes 71
Tess of the d'Urbervilles 64
Three Essays 47
Timaeus 3
To Die of Pleasure 76
Tostain, R. 21
Totem and Taboo 79
trauma 36
Turner, W. 41
Twilight 68–69, 74, 78–79

unconscious 4–6, 8, 11, 15–17
unconscious causality 9, 15
unconscious conflicts 16
unconscious constellations 17
unconscious inscriptions 9
unconscious signifiers 18

Valas, P. 16
"vamp" 76
Vampyr 76
vegetarian vampire 69
"venom" 69
Verhaeghe, P. 35, 37, 40, 49
Vienna Psychoanalytic Society 19, 29
voluptuous nightmares 71–72

wandering desire 3
wandering uterus 3
wandering womb 3
White, J. 49
Wilson, J. A. 35